ATLASES OF THE WORLD

ATLAS OF
ASIA

RUSTY CAMPBELL, MALCOLM PORTER, and KEITH LYE

rosen publishing's
rosen
central

This edition published in 2010 by:

The Rosen Publishing Group, Inc.
29 East 21st Street
New York, NY 10010

Copyright © 2010 Malcolm Porter and AS Publishing.

Additional end matter copyright © 2010 by
The Rosen Publishing Group, Inc.

Library of Congress Cataloging-in-Publication Data

Campbell, Rusty.
  Atlas of Asia / Rusty Campbell, Malcolm Porter,
    and Keith Lye.
    p. cm. – (Atlases of the world)
  Includes index.

  ISBN 978-1-4358-8455-7 (library binding)
  ISBN 978-1-4358-9112-8 (pbk.)
  ISBN 978-1-4358-9118-0 (6-pack)

  1. Asia–Maps. I. Porter, Malcolm. II. Lye, Keith.
    III. Rosen Central (Firm) IV. Title.

  G2200.C3 2010
  912.5–dc22

                                        2009582099

Manufactured in China

This edition published under license from
Cherrytree Books.

CPSIA Compliance Information: Batch #EW0102YA: For Further Information
contact Rosen Publishing, New York, New York at 1-800-237-9932

ATLASES OF THE WORLD

ATLAS OF ASIA

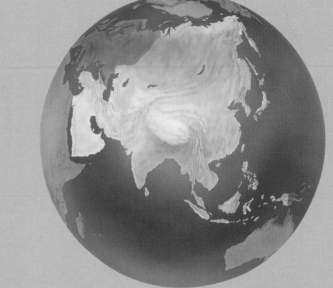

This illustrated atlas combines maps, pictures, flags, globes, information panels, diagrams and charts to give an overview of the whole continent and a closer look at each of its countries.

COUNTRY CLOSE-UPS

Each double-page spread has these features:

Introduction The author introduces the most important facts about the country or region.

Globe A globe on which you can see the country's or region's position in the continent and the world.

Flags Every country's flag is shown.

Information panels Every country has an information panel that gives its area, population and capital, and where possible its main towns, languages, religions, government and currency.

Pictures Important features of each country are illustrated and captioned to give a flavor of the country. You can find out about physical features, famous people, ordinary people, animals, plants, places, products, and much more.

Maps Every country is shown on a clear, accurate map. To get the most from the maps it helps to know the symbols that are shown in the key on the opposite page.

Land You can see by the coloring on the map where the land is forested, frozen or desert.

Height Relief hill shading shows where the mountain ranges are. Individual mountains are marked by a triangle.

Direction All of the maps are drawn with north at the top of the page.

Scale All of the maps are drawn to scale so that you can find the distance between places in miles or kilometers.

0	200 miles
0	200 kilometers

KEY TO MAPS

INDIA	Country name
Kashmir	Region
〰	Country border
▪	More than 1 million people*
•	More than 500,000 people
·	Less than 500,000 people
□	Country capital
Hindu Kush	Mountain range
▲ *Everest* 29,029ft (8,848m)	Mountain with its height
∴ *Petra*	Archaeological site

Mekong	River
	Canal
	Lake
	Dam
	Island

	Forest
	Crops
	Dry grassland
	Desert
	Tundra
	Polar

*Population figures in all cases are estimates, based on the most recent censuses where available or a variety of other sources.

CONTINENT CLOSE-UPS

People and Beliefs Map of population densities; chart of percentage of population by country; chart of areas of countries; map and chart of religions.

Climate and Vegetation Map of vegetation from forests to deserts; chart of land use; maps of summer and winter temperatures; map of annual rainfall.

Ecology and Environment Map of environmental damage to land and sea; panels on damaging the environment, natural hazards and endangered species; map of natural hazards.

Economy Map of agricultural and industrial products; pie-chart of gross domestic product for individual countries; panel on per capita gross domestic products; map of sources of energy.

Politics and History Map of great Asian empires; panel on great events; timeline of important dates; map of important events.

CONTENTS

ASIA 4

COUNTRY CLOSE-UPS

CONTINENT CLOSE-UPS

Giant panda
see page 20

ASIA

Asia is the largest of the continents, covering about three-tenths of the world's land area. It has more people than any other continent, with about three-fifths of the world's total population. Stretching from the icy Arctic in the north to the hot and steamy equatorial lands in the south, Asia contains huge empty deserts, as well as many of the world's highest mountains and longest rivers.

A long, mainly land border in the west separates Europe from Asia. This boundary runs north-south down the Ural Mountains in Russia, along the Ural River to the Caspian Sea and then through the Caucasus Mountains to the Black Sea. About three-quarters of Russia lies in Asia, while the rest is in Europe. Small parts of four other Asian countries also lie in Europe.

Cuneiform was an early form of writing. The wedge-shaped inscriptions were used around 5,000 years ago by the ancient Sumerian people, who founded a great civilization in the Tigris-Euphrates region in what is now Iraq. Several major civilizations developed in Asia.

Religions Asia was the home of all of the world's eight major religions. Hinduism is an ancient religion of India, as also is Buddhism, which was founded about 2,500 years ago. Judaism, Christianity and Islam developed in southwest Asia. Confucianism and Taoism were originally founded in China, while Shinto is a Japanese religion.

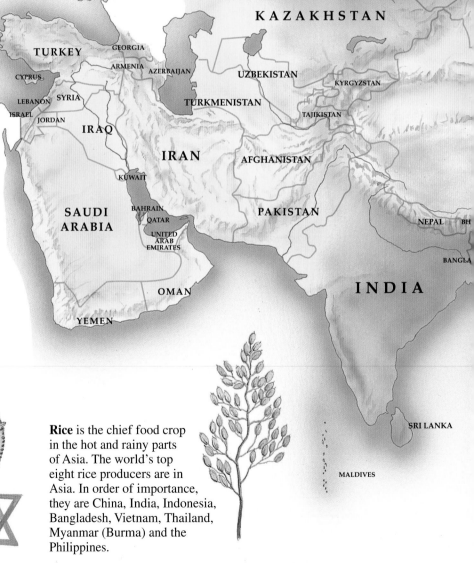

Rice is the chief food crop in the hot and rainy parts of Asia. The world's top eight rice producers are in Asia. In order of importance, they are China, India, Indonesia, Bangladesh, Vietnam, Thailand, Myanmar (Burma) and the Philippines.

ASIA

Area: 17,262,400sq miles (44,709,500sq km)
Population: 3,975,000,000
Number of independent countries: 49
(including Russia, Azerbaijan, Georgia, Kazakhstan and Turkey, which lie mostly in Asia)

S I A

MONGOLIA

NORTH
KOREA

JAPAN

SOUTH
KOREA

C H I N A

TAIWAN

YANMAR

LAOS

THAILAND   VIETNAM

PHILIPPINES

CAMBODIA

BRUNEI

MALAYSIA

SINGAPORE

I N D O N E S I A

EAST
TIMOR

Tigers live mainly in southern and southeastern Asia, but because of hunting and the destruction of the habitats where they once roamed free, they are an endangered species. Poachers kill tigers for their skins, bones and other body parts, which are used to make potions in parts of Asia.

Great Wall of China This is the longest structure ever built. It is about 4,600 miles (7,400 km) long. Construction probably began in the 5th century BCE and continued until the 17th century CE. The wall protected China from invaders from the north.

Poverty is widespread in Asia. Most countries depend on farming, but some have grown rich through manufacturing and trade. The Petronas Towers in Kuala Lumpur, Malaysia, are a symbol of Southeast Asia's increasing prosperity.

RUSSIA AND THE CAUCASUS

Russia is the world's largest country. About three-quarters of it lies in Asia, east of the Ural Mountains and the Caspian Sea. The rest is in Europe. From 1922 Russia was the center of the Communist USSR (Union of Soviet Socialist Republics), known as the Soviet Union. In 1991 the Soviet Union split up into 15 countries.

Three of these countries – Armenia, Azerbaijan and Georgia – border Russia in the southwest. Together they are called Transcaucasia after the high Caucasus Mountains that lie to the north. Conflict has occurred in Chechnya, Russia, and also in parts of Transcaucasia, as rival ethnic and religious groups have fought for independence.

Woolly mammoths lived during the Ice Age in Siberia (a name often used for Asian Russia). They died out about 10,000 years ago, but bodies of mammoths have been found perfectly preserved in the frozen subsoil of Siberia.

RUSSIA

Area: 6,592,850sq miles (17,075,400sq km), of which about 75% is in Asia
Highest point: Mount Elbrus, in the Caucasus Mountains, 18,510ft (5,642m)
Population: 142,894,000 (about 20% of whom live in Asian Russia)
Capital and largest city: Moscow (pop 10,469,000)
Other large cities (in Asian Russia):
Novosibirsk (1,426,000)
Yekaterinburg (1,290,000)
Omsk (1,130,000)
Chelyabinsk (1,058,000)
Krasnoyarsk (907,000)
Irkutsk (584,000)
Official language: Russian
Religions: Christianity (Russian Orthodox 20%), Islam 10%
Government: Republic
Currency: Ruble

Oil and natural gas are abundant in Russia, and the country is a major producer. Azerbaijan also has large oil deposits in the Caspian Sea. Russia has most of the minerals it needs, including bauxite, copper, diamonds, iron ore, nickel, and phosphates (used to make fertilizers).

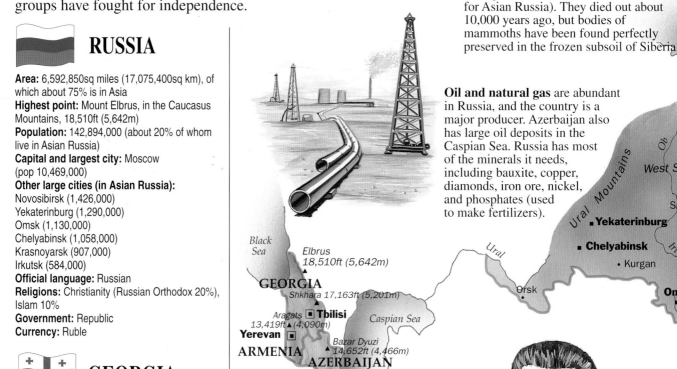

Black Sea
Elbrus 18,510ft (5,642m)
GEORGIA
Shkhara 17,163ft (5,201m)
Aragats 13,419ft (4,090m) ■ Tbilisi
Yerevan ■
ARMENIA
Bazar Dyuzi 14,652ft (4,466m)
AZERBAIJAN
■ Baku
Caspian Sea
Ural
Ural Mountains
West Sibe
Ob
■ Yekaterinburg
■ Chelyabinsk
Surgu
Irtysh
• Kurgan
Orsk
Omsk

GEORGIA

Area: 26,911sq miles (69,700sq km), 21% of which is in Europe
Highest point: Mt Shkhara 17,163ft (5,201m)
Population: 4,661,000
Capital: Tbilisi (pop 1,064,000)
Official language: Georgian
Religions: Christianity (84%), Islam (10%)
Government: Republic
Currency: Lari

ARMENIA

Area: 11,506sq miles (29,800sq km)
Highest point: Mt Aragats 13,419ft (4,090m)
Population: 2,976,000
Capital: Yerevan (pop 1,079,000)
Official language: Armenian
Religions: Christianity (Armenian Apostolic 95%, other Christian 4%)
Government: Republic
Currency: Dram

AZERBAIJAN

Area: 33,436sq miles (86,600sq km), 17% of which is in Europe
Highest point: Bazar Dyuzi 14,652ft (4,466m)
Population: 7,962,000
Capital: Baku (pop 1,816,000)
Official language: Azerbaijani
Religion: Islam (93%)
Government: Republic
Currency: Manat

Joseph Stalin (1879-1953) was born in Georgia. He played a leading part in the 1917 Russian Revolution, which turned Russia into a Communist country. From 1929 until his death in 1953, Stalin was the dictator of the Soviet Union. His rule was marked by great brutality.

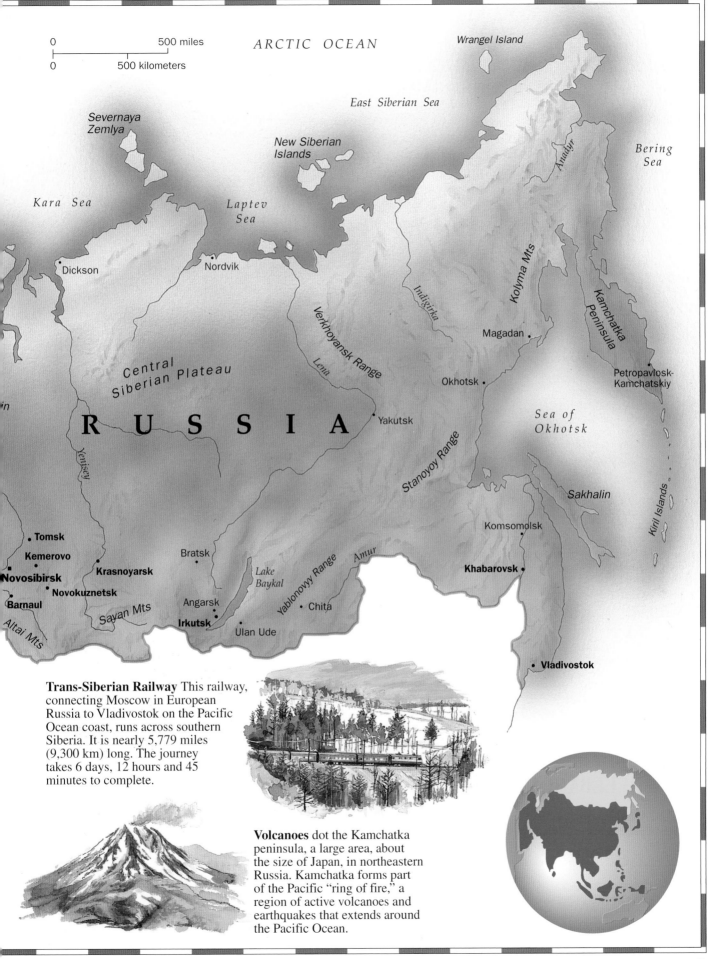

0 — 500 miles
0 — 500 kilometers

ARCTIC OCEAN

Wrangel Island

East Siberian Sea

Severnaya Zemlya

New Siberian Islands

Bering Sea

Kara Sea

Laptev Sea

Anadyr

• Dickson

• Nordvik

Kolyma Mts

Indigirka

Kamchatka Peninsula

Verkhoyansk Range

• Magadan

Central Siberian Plateau

Lena

R U S S I A

• Yakutsk

• Okhotsk

Petropavlosk-Kamchatskiy

Sea of Okhotsk

Yenisey

Stanovoy Range

Sakhalin

Kuril Islands

• Komsomolsk

Tomsk

Kemerovo

Bratsk

Lake Baykal

Khabarovsk •

Novosibirsk

Krasnoyarsk

Yablonovyy Range

Amur

Novokuznetsk

Angarsk

• Chita

Barnaul

Sayan Mts

Irkutsk

Ulan Ude

Altai Mts

Vladivostok

Trans-Siberian Railway This railway, connecting Moscow in European Russia to Vladivostok on the Pacific Ocean coast, runs across southern Siberia. It is nearly 5,779 miles (9,300 km) long. The journey takes 6 days, 12 hours and 45 minutes to complete.

Volcanoes dot the Kamchatka peninsula, a large area, about the size of Japan, in northeastern Russia. Kamchatka forms part of the Pacific "ring of fire," a region of active volcanoes and earthquakes that extends around the Pacific Ocean.

MEDITERRANEAN ASIA

At the eastern end of the Mediterranean Sea lies a group of six Asian countries. The largest is Turkey, a small part of which lies in Europe, west of the waterway linking the Mediterranean and Black seas. Turkey is a largely mountainous country with a mild, rainy climate. Cyprus and Lebanon have pleasant sunny climates, but hot deserts cover much of Israel, Jordan and Syria.

Israel was founded as a Jewish state in the ancient region of Palestine in 1948, but it has had to fight for its existence against its Arab neighbors in wars in 1948-9, 1956, 1967 and 1973. In 1967 it gained large areas from Egypt, Jordan and Syria.

TURKEY

Area: 299,158sq miles (774,815sq km), 97% of which is in Asia
Highest point: Mt Ararat 17,011ft (5,185m)
Population: 70,414,000
Capital: Ankara (pop 3,428,000)
Official language: Turkish
Religion: Islam
Government: Republic
Currency: Turkish lira

CYPRUS

Area: 3,572sq miles (9,251sq km)
Highest point: Mt Olympus 6,403ft (1,952m)
Population: 784,000
Capital: Nicosia (pop 205,000)
Official languages: Greek, Turkish
Religions: Greek Orthodox (78%), Islam (18%)
Government: Republic
Currency: Cyprus pound, Turkish new lira

SYRIA

Area: 71,498sq miles (185,180sq km)
Highest point: Mt Hermon 9,232ft (2,814m)
Population: 18,881,000
Capital: Damascus (pop 2,228,000)
Official language: Arabic
Religion: Islam (90%)
Government: Republic
Currency: Syrian pound

LEBANON

Area: 4,015sq miles (10,400sq km)
Highest point: Qurnat as Sawda 10,115ft (3,083m)
Population: 3,874,000
Capital: Beirut (pop 1,792,000)
Official language: Arabic
Religions: Islam (60%), Christianity (39%)
Government: Republic
Currency: Lebanese pound

Earthquakes occur in northern Turkey as the land moves along huge faults (cracks) in the earth's crust. At least 13,000 people died in 1999 when an earthquake struck the area near Izmit in northwestern Turkey.

ISRAEL

Area: 8,130sq miles (21,056sq km)
Highest point: Mt Meron 3,963 (1,208m ft)
Population: 6,352,000
Capital: Jerusalem (pop 686,000)
Official languages: Hebrew, Arabic
Religions: Judaism (80%), Islam (15%)
Government: Republic
Currency: New sheqel

JORDAN

Area: 37,738sq miles (97,740sq km)
Highest point: Jabal Ramm 5,755ft (1,754m)
Population: 5,907,000
Capital: Amman (pop 1,237,000)
Official language: Arabic
Religions: Islam (94%), Christianity (6%)
Government: Monarchy
Currency: Jordan dinar

Jerusalem is a holy city for Christians, Jews and Muslims. From 1949, Israel controlled western Jerusalem and made it their capital in 1950. Eastern Jerusalem was held by Lebanon until Israeli forces captured eastern Jerusalem during the 1967 Arab-Israeli War. Here devout Jews pray at the Wailing Wall, a sacred place of Judaism.

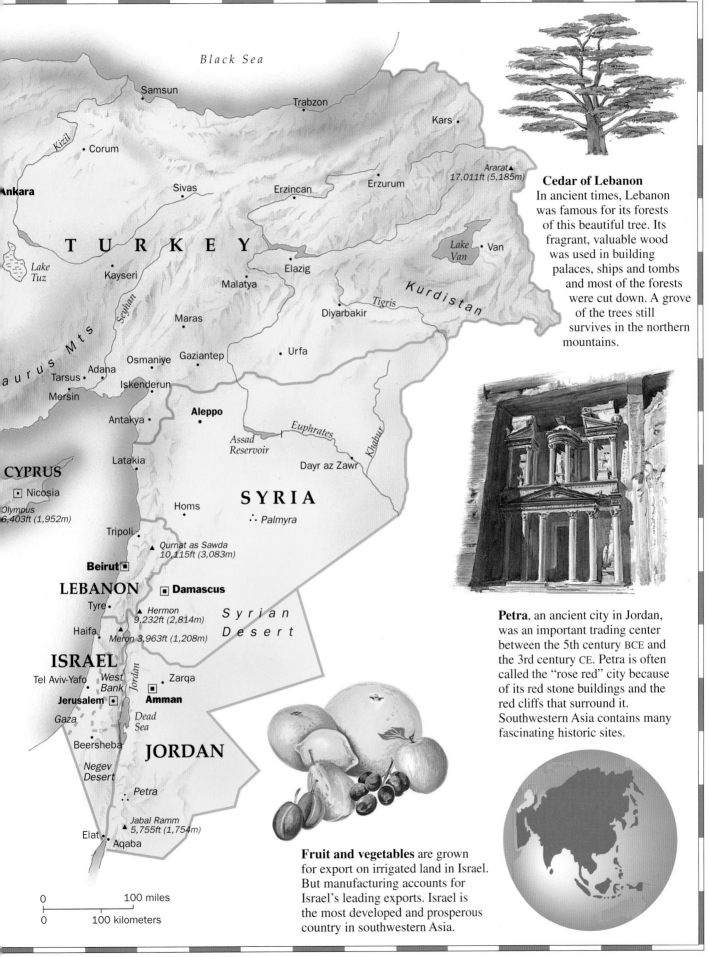

Black Sea

Samsun
Trabzon
Kars
Corum
Kizil
Ankara
Sivas
Erzincan
Erzurum
Ararat▲
17,011ft (5,185m)

T U R K E Y

Lake
Tuz
Kayseri
Malatya
Elazig
Lake
Van
• Van

Kurdistan

Seyhan
Tigris
Diyarbakir

Taurus Mts
Maras

Osmaniye
Gaziantep
• Urfa
Adana
Tarsus
Iskenderun
Mersin

Antakya •
Aleppo
Euphrates

Assad
Reservoir
Khabur

CYPRUS
Latakia
Dayr az Zawr

□ Nicosia
S Y R I A

Olympus
6,403ft (1,952m)
Homs
∴ Palmyra

Tripoli •
▲ Qurnat as Sawda
10,115ft (3,083m)

Beirut ▣

LEBANON
▣ **Damascus**
Tyre •
▲ Hermon
9,232ft (2,814m)
S y r i a n
D e s e r t

Haifa •
▲
Meron 3,963ft (1,208m)

ISRAEL
Jordan
Tel Aviv-Yafo •
West
Bank
• Zarqa

Jerusalem ▣
▣ **Amman**

Gaza
Dead
Sea

Beersheba •
JORDAN

Negev
Desert

∴ Petra

Jabal Ramm
▲ 5,755ft (1,754m)

Elat •
Aqaba •

0 ___ 100 miles
0 ___ 100 kilometers

Cedar of Lebanon
In ancient times, Lebanon
was famous for its forests
of this beautiful tree. Its
fragrant, valuable wood
was used in building
palaces, ships and tombs
and most of the forests
were cut down. A grove
of the trees still
survives in the northern
mountains.

Petra, an ancient city in Jordan,
was an important trading center
between the 5th century BCE and
the 3rd century CE. Petra is often
called the "rose red" city because
of its red stone buildings and the
red cliffs that surround it.
Southwestern Asia contains many
fascinating historic sites.

Fruit and vegetables are grown
for export on irrigated land in Israel.
But manufacturing accounts for
Israel's leading exports. Israel is
the most developed and prosperous
country in southwestern Asia.

9

ARABIAN PENINSULA

The Arabian peninsula lies between the Red Sea and The Gulf (also known as the Arabian or Persian Gulf). Hot, thinly populated deserts cover most of the peninsula. Farming is possible only around oases where people can get water from underground rocks. But Bahrain, Oman, Qatar, Saudi Arabia and United Arab Emirates all have rich oil reserves. Yemen is the poorest country in this region.

Mecca in Saudi Arabia was the birthplace of the Prophet Mohammed (? 570-632 CE), who founded the religion of Islam. Every year more than a million Muslims from all over the world visit Mecca on a pilgrimage called the hajj.

SAUDI ARABIA

Area: 830,000sq miles (2,149,690sq km)
Highest point: Abha 10,279ft (3,139m)
Population: 27,020,000
Capital: Riyadh (pop 5,126,000)
Official language: Arabic
Religion: Islam
Government: Monarchy
Currency: Saudi riyal

YEMEN

Area: 203,850sq miles (527,968sq km)
Highest point: Hadur Shuayb 12,336ft (3,760m)
Population: 21,456,000
Capital: Sana (pop 1,469,000)
Official language: Arabic
Religion: Islam
Government: Republic
Currency: Yemeni rial

Arabian oryx This graceful antelope was almost extinct in the Arabian peninsula until some were taken to Phoenix Zoo, Arizona. There, a world herd was established. Animals from this herd have been released in Jordan, Oman and Saudi Arabia.

Muslim women often follow the *hijab* dress code by wearing a simple scarf. Others cover their face with the *niqab*. This form of clothing is required by strict Muslim teachings, but women in some Muslim countries wear western dress.

OMAN

Area: 82,030sq miles (212,457sq km)
Highest point: Jabal Ash Sham 9,957ft (3,035m)
Population: 3,102,000
Capital: Muscat (pop 638,000)
Official language: Arabic
Religions: Islam (88%), Hinduism (7%)
Government: Monarchy
Currency: Omani rial

QATAR

Area: 4,247sq miles (11,000sq km)
Population: 885,000
Capital: Doha (pop 286,000)
Official language: Arabic
Religion: Islam (95%)
Government: Monarchy
Currency: Qatar riyal

UNITED ARAB EMIRATES

Area: 32,278sq miles (83,600sq km)
Highest point: Jabal Yibir 5,010ft (1,527m)
Population: 2,603,000
Capital: Abu Dhabi (pop 475,000)
Official language: Arabic
Religion: Islam (96%)
Government: Federation of seven emirates
Currency: UAE dirham

BAHRAIN

Area: 268sq miles (694sq km)
Population: 699,000
Capital: Manama (pop 139,000)
Official language: Arabic
Religions: Islam (80%), Christianity (9%)
Government: Monarchy
Currency: Bahrain dinar

Al Jawf

Tabuk

An Nafud

Al Wajh

Medina

Yanbu

Jiddah

Mecca

At Taif

Red Sea

Rub al Khali This bleak desert lies mainly in southern Saudi Arabia and also in Yemen. It is often called the "Empty Quarter" because it contains the world's largest expanse of sand. Plants are almost nonexistent, growing only at oases.

Dates are the nutritious fruits of the date palm, the commonest tree in the Arabian peninsula. The tree trunks are used in building and the leaves are used to make baskets and mats. Dates have been an important food in southwestern Asia for at least 5,000 years.

Camels can travel long distances without having to drink water. They are often called the "ships of the desert" because they were the traditional means of transporting people and goods across deserts.

Hafar

Buraydah

The Gulf

Damman

BAHRAIN

Manama

QATAR

Al Hufuf

Doha

Riyadh

Haradh

SAUDI ARABIA

Sharjah

Dubai

Abu Dhabi

UNITED ARAB
EMIRATES

Strait of Hormuz

OMAN

Jabal Yibir
5,010ft
(1,527m)

Gulf of
Oman

Al Khaburah

Muscat

Jabal Ash Sham
9,957ft (3,035m)

R u b   a l   K h a l i

(Empty Quarter)

OMAN

Al Masira

Dhufar

,279ft (3,139m)
oha

Hadhramaut

Salalah

Arabian Sea

Sana

Hadur Shuayb 12,336ft (3,760m)

Al Hudaydah

Zabid

YEMEN

Al Mukalla

Taiz

Mocha

Aden

0		200 miles
0		200 kilometers

Oil tankers transport oil from the Gulf region all around the world. Saudi Arabia is the largest producer and exporter of oil and it has the world's largest known reserves. Money from oil sales has been used to develop industries and welfare services in the Arabian peninsula.

IRAQ, IRAN AND KUWAIT

Iraq contains large deserts but also has a fertile region called Mesopotamia. Mesopotamia means "the land between the rivers." The rivers are the Tigris and Euphrates, which rise in Turkey and flow across Iraq. Mesopotamia was the place where Sumer, the oldest known civilization, developed. Later civilizations in Mesopotamia included those of Assyria and Babylon. Iran (formerly Persia) also has many magnificent historic sites, including the ancient city of Persepolis, which was destroyed by Alexander the Great.

Since the 1980s, these oil-rich, Muslim countries have been at war. Iran and Iraq fought between 1980 and 1988. In 1990 Iraq invaded Kuwait and an allied force led by the United States drove Iraqi troops out of Kuwait. A second invasion in 2003 deposed Iraq's dictator Saddam Hussein and elections for a new government were held in 2005. But violence continued and many Iraqis have become refugees.

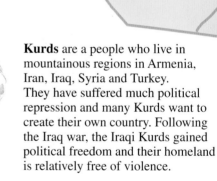

IRAQ

Area: 169,235sq miles (438,317sq km)
Highest point: 11,480ft (3,609m) in Zagros Mts
Population: 26,500,000
Capital and largest city: Baghdad (pop 5,500,000)
Other large cities: Mosul, Irbil, Basra
(no reliable figures available)
Official languages: Arabic, Kurdish
Religions: Islam (97%), Christianity (3%)
Government: Republic
Currency: New Iraqi dinar

IRAN

Area: 642,161sq miles (1,633,188sq km)
Highest point: Mt Damavand 18,386ft (5,604m)
Population: 68,688,000
Capital and largest city: Tehran (pop 7,190,000)
Other large cities: Mashhad (1,990,000)
Tabriz (1,461,000)
Esfahan (1,381,000)
Official language: Farsi (Persian)
Religion: Islam (99%)
Government: Islamic republic
Currency: Iranian rial

KUWAIT

Area: 6,880sq miles (17,818sq km)
Population: 2,418,000
Capital: Kuwait (pop 1,222,000)
Official language: Arabic
Religion: Islam (85%)
Government: Monarchy
Currency: Kuwaiti dinar

Kurds are a people who live in mountainous regions in Armenia, Iran, Iraq, Syria and Turkey. They have suffered much political repression and many Kurds want to create their own country. Following the Iraq war, the Iraqi Kurds gained political freedom and their homeland is relatively free of violence.

Ur was a city in ancient Sumer, identified in the Bible as the home of Abraham. The people of Sumer built temples that stood on the top of pyramid-like structures, called *ziggurats*.

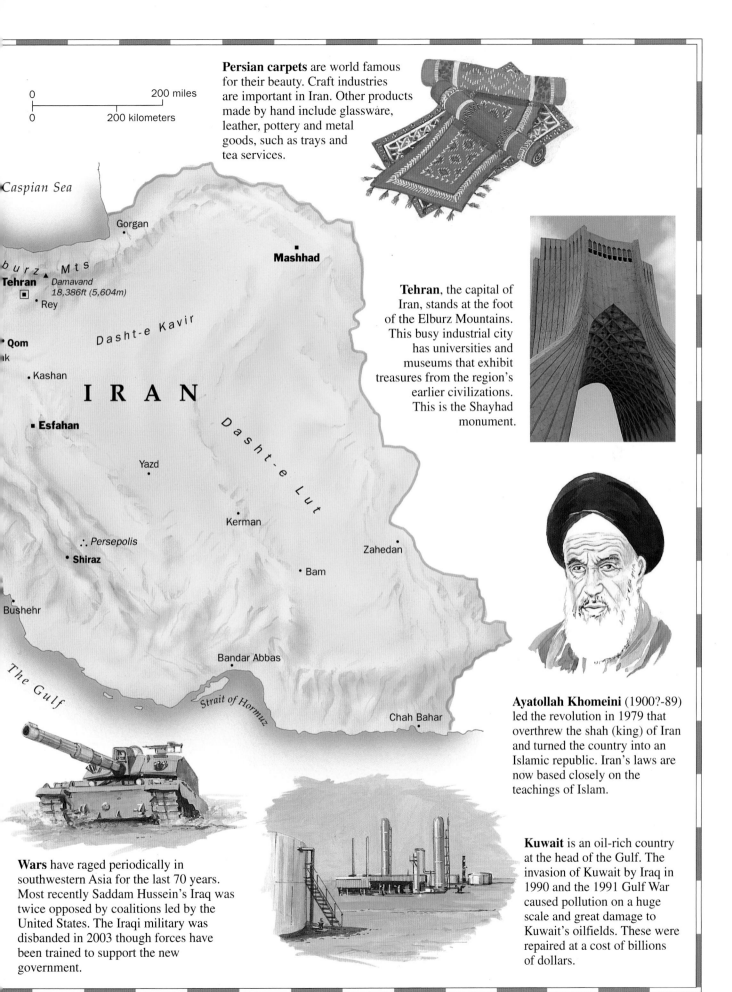

Persian carpets are world famous for their beauty. Craft industries are important in Iran. Other products made by hand include glassware, leather, pottery and metal goods, such as trays and tea services.

0 —————————— 200 miles
0 —————————— 200 kilometers

Caspian Sea

Gorgan

Mashhad

burz Mts

Tehran ▲ *Damavand*
■ *18,386ft (5,604m)*
• Rey

Tehran, the capital of Iran, stands at the foot of the Elburz Mountains. This busy industrial city has universities and museums that exhibit treasures from the region's earlier civilizations. This is the Shayhad monument.

• Qom
ak

Dasht-e Kavir

• Kashan

I R A N

Esfahan

Dasht-e Lut

Yazd

Kerman

∴ *Persepolis*
• **Shiraz**

Zahedan

• Bam

Bushehr

The Gulf

Bandar Abbas

Strait of Hormuz

Chah Bahar

Ayatollah Khomeini (1900?-89) led the revolution in 1979 that overthrew the shah (king) of Iran and turned the country into an Islamic republic. Iran's laws are now based closely on the teachings of Islam.

Wars have raged periodically in southwestern Asia for the last 70 years. Most recently Saddam Hussein's Iraq was twice opposed by coalitions led by the United States. The Iraqi military was disbanded in 2003 though forces have been trained to support the new government.

Kuwait is an oil-rich country at the head of the Gulf. The invasion of Kuwait by Iraq in 1990 and the 1991 Gulf War caused pollution on a huge scale and great damage to Kuwait's oilfields. These were repaired at a cost of billions of dollars.

CENTRAL ASIA

The five countries of Central Asia were once part of the Soviet Union. They became independent in 1991, when the Soviet Union split up. Kazakhstan, the world's ninth largest country, lies mainly in Asia, though a small area in the west lies in Europe.

Central Asia contains mountains, deserts, huge lakes and vast grassy plains called steppes. Attempts to develop the land have created environmental problems. Much of the river water that once flowed into the Aral Sea, for example, is now used by farmers and the huge lake has shrunk. Areas that were once fishing grounds are now desert.

KAZAKHSTAN

Area: 1,049,040sq miles (2,717,000sq km), 4% of which is in Europe
Highest point: Mt Teneri 20,991ft (6,398m)
Population: 15,233,000
Capital: Astana (pop 332,000)
Official language: Kazakh
Religions: Islam (47%), Christianity (10%)
Government: Republic
Currency: Tenge

UZBEKISTAN

Area: 172,742sq miles (447,400sq km)
Highest point: 15,233ft (4,643m) in the southeast
Population: 27,307,000
Capital: Tashkent (pop 2,155,000)
Official language: Uzbek
Religion: Islam (88%)
Government: Republic
Currency: Uzbekistani som

TURKMENISTAN

Area: 188,546sq miles (488,100sq km)
Highest point: Kugitangtau 10,292ft (3,137m)
Population: 5,043,000
Capital: Ashgabat (pop 574,000)
Official language: Turkmen
Religion: Islam (89%)
Government: Republic
Currency: Manat

TAJIKISTAN

Area: 56,023sq miles (145,100sq km)
Highest point: Ismoili Somoni 24,590ft (7,495m)
Population: 7,321,000
Capital: Dushanbe (pop 554,000)
Official language: Tajik
Religion: Islam (85%)
Government: Republic
Currency: Somoni

Cotton is a major crop throughout Central Asia and agriculture is the main activity. The governments of these former Communist countries have been working since 1991 to introduce private ownership of the land and industries.

KYRGYZSTAN

Area: 76,641sq miles (198,500sq km)
Highest point: Jengish Chokusu 24,406ft (7,439m)
Population: 5,214,000
Capital: Bishkek (pop 806,000)
Official language: Kyrgyz
Religion: Islam (75%)
Government: Republic
Currency: Kyrgyzstani som

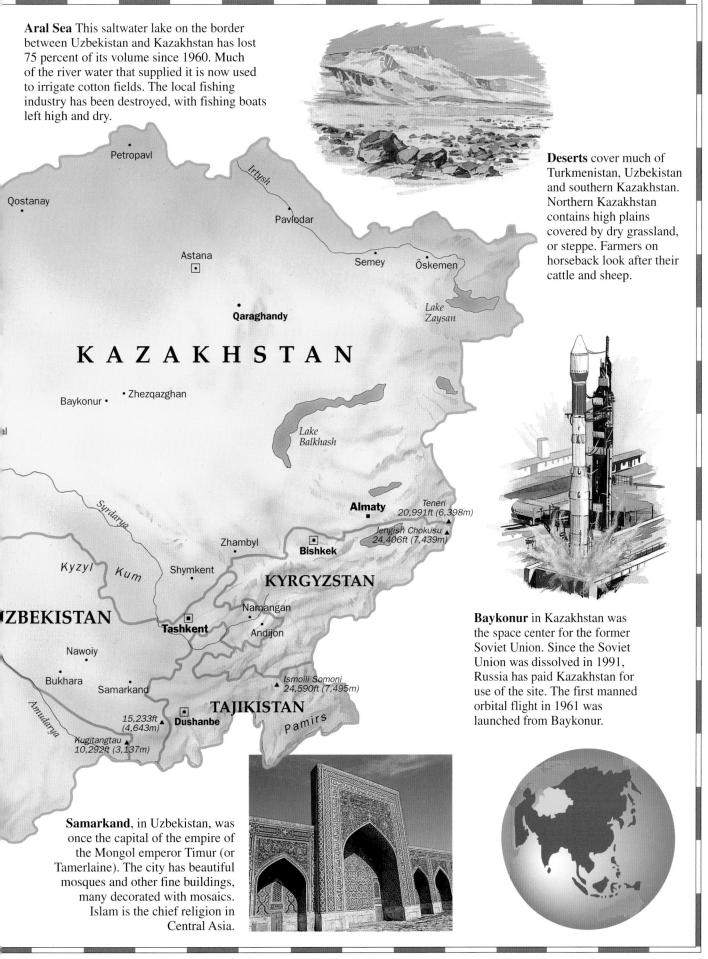

Aral Sea This saltwater lake on the border between Uzbekistan and Kazakhstan has lost 75 percent of its volume since 1960. Much of the river water that supplied it is now used to irrigate cotton fields. The local fishing industry has been destroyed, with fishing boats left high and dry.

Deserts cover much of Turkmenistan, Uzbekistan and southern Kazakhstan. Northern Kazakhstan contains high plains covered by dry grassland, or steppe. Farmers on horseback look after their cattle and sheep.

Baykonur in Kazakhstan was the space center for the former Soviet Union. Since the Soviet Union was dissolved in 1991, Russia has paid Kazakhstan for use of the site. The first manned orbital flight in 1961 was launched from Baykonur.

Samarkand, in Uzbekistan, was once the capital of the empire of the Mongol emperor Timur (or Tamerlaine). The city has beautiful mosques and other fine buildings, many decorated with mosaics. Islam is the chief religion in Central Asia.

Petropavl

Qostanay

Irtysh

Pavlodar

Astana

Semey

Öskemen

Qaraghandy

KAZAKHSTAN

Lake Zaysan

Baykonur •

• Zhezqazghan

Lake Balkhash

Almaty

Teneri 20,991ft (6,398m)

Jengish Chokusu ▲ 24,406ft (7,439m)

Syrdarya

Bishkek

Zhambyl

Shymkent

KYRGYZSTAN

Kyzyl Kum

Namangan

UZBEKISTAN

Tashkent

Andijon

Nawoiy

Ismoili Somoni ▲ 24,590ft (7,495m)

Bukhara

Samarkand

TAJIKISTAN

Amudarya

15,233ft (4,643m) ▲ **Dushanbe**

Pamirs

Kugitangtau ▲ 10,292ft (3,137m)

AFGHANISTAN AND PAKISTAN

Landlocked Afghanistan is one of the world's poorest countries. Highlands and mountains cover most of the land. Afghanistan has suffered drought, famine and wars. In 1989 a Russian occupation force was ousted. By 1996 most of the country had fallen under the control of the Taliban, a strict Muslim group. In 2001 the Taliban were accused of aiding Al Qaeda terrorists, and a US-led invasion overthrew them. An elected government was set up, but fighting continued and many Afghans became refugees.

   Pakistan has high mountains but also fertile plains drained by the Indus River and its tributaries. Pakistan became independent in 1947, when it broke away from British India. It remains in dispute with India over the region of Kashmir.

 **AFGHANISTAN**

Area: 251,773sq miles (652,090sq km)
Highest point: Nowshak, in the Hindu Kush, 24,557ft (7,485m)
Population: 31,057,000
Capital and largest city: Kabul (pop 2,956,000)
Other large cities: Kandahar (401,000)
Mazar-e-Sharif (315,000)
Herat (278,000)
Jalalabad (209,000)
Official languages: Dari (Persian), Pashto
Religion: Islam
Government: Republic
Currency: Afghani

 **PAKISTAN**

Area: 307,374sq miles (796,095sq km)
Highest point: K2 28,250ft (8,611m)
Population: 165,804,000
Capital: Islamabad (pop 698,000)
Largest cities: Karachi (10,032,000)
Lahore (5,452,000)
Faisalabad (2,582,000)
Rawalpindi (1,793,000)
Gujranwala (1,421,000)
Hyderabad (1,417,000)
Official language: Urdu
Religion: Islam (95%)
Government: Military regime
Currency: Pakistani rupee

Muslims pray five times a day, at dawn, noon, in the afternoon and evening, and finally at nightfall. When they pray, they always face Mecca, the birthplace of the Prophet Mohammed. Afghanistan and Pakistan are both Islamic states.

Fruits of many kinds are grown in Afghanistan and Pakistan. The economies of both countries depend on agriculture. Wheat is their chief food crop. Many farmers raise goats and sheep. Manufacturing is increasing in Pakistan.

Herat

Harirud

AFGHANISTAN

Helmand

Kandahar

Rigestan Desert

Baluchistan Plateau

Gwadar

Arabian Sea

0   100 miles
0   100 kilometers

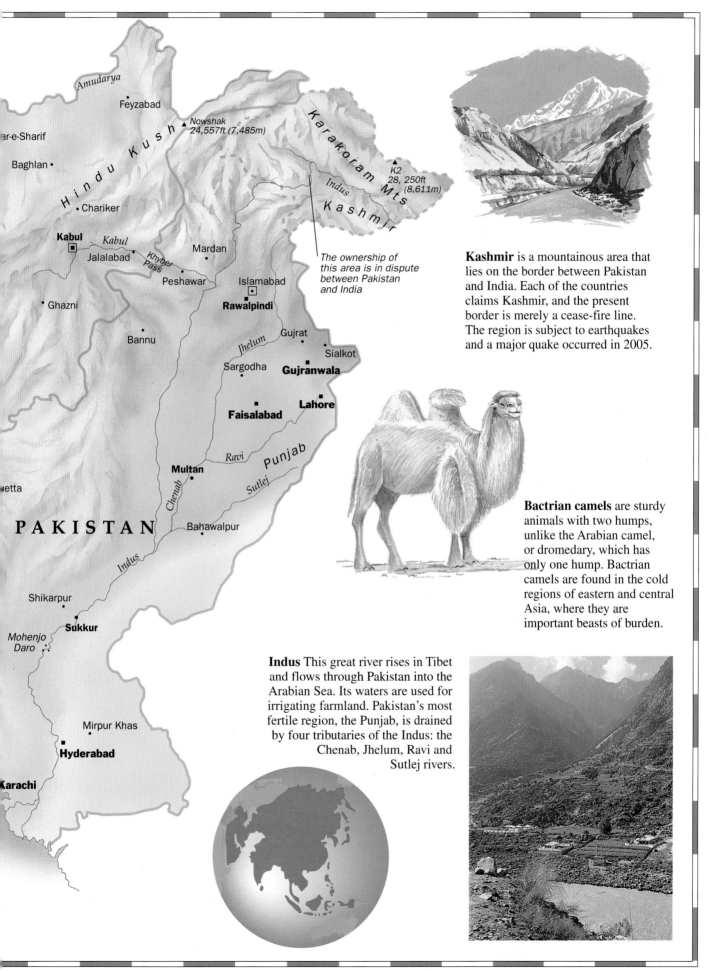

Feyzabad

Amudarya

ar-e-Sharif

Baghlan

Hindu Kush

Nowshak
24,557ft (7,485m)

Karakoram Mts

K2
28, 250ft
(8,611m)

Indus

Kashmir

Chariker

Kabul

Kabul

Jalalabad

Khyber Pass

Mardan

Peshawar

Islamabad

Ghazni

Rawalpindi

The ownership of
this area is in dispute
between Pakistan
and India

Bannu

Jhelum

Gujrat

Sialkot

Sargodha

Gujranwala

Lahore

Faisalabad

Ravi

Punjab

Multan

Chenab

Sutlej

Quetta

P A K I S T A N

Bahawalpur

Indus

Shikarpur

Sukkur

Mohenjo
Daro

Mirpur Khas

Hyderabad

Karachi

Kashmir is a mountainous area that
lies on the border between Pakistan
and India. Each of the countries
claims Kashmir, and the present
border is merely a cease-fire line.
The region is subject to earthquakes
and a major quake occurred in 2005.

Bactrian camels are sturdy
animals with two humps,
unlike the Arabian camel,
or dromedary, which has
only one hump. Bactrian
camels are found in the cold
regions of eastern and central
Asia, where they are
important beasts of burden.

Indus This great river rises in Tibet
and flows through Pakistan into the
Arabian Sea. Its waters are used for
irrigating farmland. Pakistan's most
fertile region, the Punjab, is drained
by four tributaries of the Indus: the
Chenab, Jhelum, Ravi and
Sutlej rivers.

INDIAN SUBCONTINENT

India is the world's seventh largest country, but in population it ranks second only to China. Northern India is mountainous, and long rivers, including the Ganges, flow down from the mountains and across the fertile plains to the south of the mountains. South India is a tableland called the Deccan. India became independent from Britain in 1947.

The Indian subcontinent also includes Bhutan and Nepal, two mountainous countries in the Himalaya region, and the beautiful island country of Sri Lanka (formerly called Ceylon), which lies off the southern tip of India. The Maldives is an island nation lying to the southwest of southern India. A tsunami in 2004 struck the coasts of India, the Maldives and Sri Lanka.

INDIA

Area: 1,269,346sq miles (3,287,590sq km)
Highest point: Kanchenjunga 28,208ft (8,598m)
Population: 1,095,352,000
Capital: New Delhi (pop 301,000)
Largest cities: Mumbai (formerly Bombay, 16,086,000)
Kolkata (Calcutta, 13,058,000)
Delhi (12,441,000)
Chennai (Madras, 6,353,000)
Official languages: Hindi, English
Religions: Hinduism (81%), Islam (13%),
Government: Federal republic
Currency: Indian rupee

SRI LANKA

Area: 25,332sq miles (65,610sq km)
Highest point: Pidurutalagala 8,281ft (2,524m)
Population: 20,222,000
Capital: Colombo (pop 648,000)
Official languages: Sinhala, Tamil
Religions: Buddhism (69%), Hinduism (7%), Islam (7%), Christianity (6%)
Government: Republic
Currency: Sri Lankan rupee

NEPAL

Area: 56,827sq miles (147,181sq km)
Highest point: Mt Everest 29,029ft (8,848m)
Population: 28,287,000
Capital: Kathmandu (pop 741,000)
Other large cities: Lalitpur (189,000)
Official language: Nepali
Religions: Hinduism (85%), Buddhism (11%)
Government: Monarchy
Currency: Nepalese rupee

MALDIVES

Area: 115sq miles (298sq km)
Highest point: 80ft (24m) on Wilingili Island west of Male
Population: 359,000
Capital: Male (pop 83,000)
Official language: Dhivehi
Religion: Islam
Government: Republic
Currency: Maldivian rufiyaa

BHUTAN

Area: 18,147sq miles (47,000sq km)
Highest point: Kula Kangri 24,783ft (7,554m)
Population: 672,000
Capital: Thimphu (pop 35,000)
Official language: Dzongkha
Religions: Buddhism (75%), Hinduism (25%)
Government: Monarchy
Currency: Ngultrum

0   200 miles

0   200 kilometers

Srinagar   Leh

Jammu

Amritsar

Jullundur

Ludhiana   Chandigarh

Dehra Dun

Delhi   Meerut

Bikaner   New Delhi   Bare

Aligarh

Great Indian (Thar) Desert

Jaipur   Luckn

Ajmer   Agra   Kanpur

Jodhpur

Gwalior

Kota

Ahmadabad   Ujjain   Bhopal

Indore

Jamnagar   Rajkot   Vadodara   *Narmada*

Bhavnagar   Nagpur

Surat

Arabian Sea   Aurangabad   **I N D I A**

Mumbai   *Godavari*

Pune   Warar

Sholapur

Deccan Plateau

Hyderabad

Goa

Mangalore   Bangalore   Che

Mysore

Salem

Kozhikode   Tiruchchirap

Coimbatore

Cochin   Madurai

Tirunelveli

Thiruvananthapuram

MALDIVES   *INDIAN OCEAN*

Male

Himalayas The Himalayas is a range of mountains that borders the Indian subcontinent in the north. It contains the world's highest peak, Mount Everest, which stands on the border between Nepal and China. Bhutan also contains part of the Himalayas.

NEPAL
Everest ▲
29,029ft (8,848m) *Kanchenjunga*
28,208ft (8,598m)
Kathmandu •
Lalitpur •
Darjiling •
▲ *Kula Kangri*
24,783ft (7,554m)
• **BHUTAN**
Thimphu •
Brahmaputra
A S

• Gorakhpur
• Guwahati
zabad
abad •
Patna
Bhagalpur •
• Imphal
Ganges
Varanasi
Asanol •
Ranchi •
Jamshedpur •
Kolkata
Haora •
Bilaspur
aipur
Cuttack •
Bay of Bengal
h a t s
• Vishakhapatnam
ayawada

Mohandas Gandhi (1869-1948) was a great political and spiritual leader in India. People called him the *Mahatma*, a title meaning "Great Soul." Gandhi helped to free India from Britain, using nonviolent resistance to oppose the government. He was assassinated in 1948.

Hindu gods are believed by most Hindus to be different aspects of the one god Brahman. Statues like this one are placed in temples and homes. Hindu beliefs and practices vary throughout India and worshippers celebrate many festivals.

Taj Mahal One of the world's most famous and beautiful buildings, the Taj Mahal is in Agra, northwestern India. It was built between 1630 and 1650 by an Indian ruler, Shah Jehan, as a tomb for his beloved wife, Mumtaz Mahal.

RI LANKA
Pidurutalagala
▲ 8,281ft (2,524m)
ombo
na

Tea India and Sri Lanka are among the world's leading tea producers. India's chief food crops are rice and wheat. India has more cattle than any other country but Hindus do not eat meat. They regard cattle as sacred animals.

CHINA, MONGOLIA AND TAIWAN

China is the world's third largest country after Russia and Canada, but in population it ranks first. China includes Hong Kong, a former British territory that was returned to China in 1997, and Macau, a former Portuguese territory that was returned in 1999. China also claims the island of Taiwan, but the Taiwanese do not want to be ruled by the Communist government of China.

China became a Communist country in 1949, but since the late 1970s it has been changing. The government has encouraged private ownership of land and invited foreign companies to invest in new industries in eastern China. By 2006 China had the world's fourth largest economy, though millions of Chinese still live in poverty.

CHINA

Area: 3,691,938sq miles (9,562,074sq km)
Highest point: Mt Everest 29,029ft (8,848m)
Population: 1,313,974,000
Capital: Beijing (pop 10,848,000)
Other large cities: Shanghai (12,837,000)
Tianjin (9,156,000)
Shenyang (4,828,000)
Chongqing (4,635,000)
Wuhan (4,236,000)
Official language: Mandarin Chinese
Religions: Chinese folk religions (20%),
Buddhism (8%), Christianity (6%)
Government: People's republic
Currency: Yuan (Renminbi)

MONGOLIA

Area: 604,829sq miles (1,566,500sq km)
Highest point: 14,311ft (4,362m) in the Altai Mts
Population: 2,832,000
Capital: Ulan Bator (pop 812,000)
Official language: Khalkha Mongolian
Religions: Lamaism, a kind of Buddhism, (50%),
Islam (4%)
Government: Republic
Currency: Tugrik (Togrog)

TAIWAN

Area: 13,892sq miles (35,980sq km)
Highest point: Tu Shan 13,113ft (3,997m)
Population: 23,036,000
Capital: Taipei (pop 2,550,000)
Official language Mandarin Chinese, Taiwa nese
Religions: Traditional beliefs embracing
Buddhism, Confucianism and Taoism
Government: Republic
Currency: New Taiwan dollar

Giant panda This endangered animal is the symbol used by WWF (World Wildlife Fund). In the wild, pandas are found in only a few remaining bamboo forests on mountain slopes in western and southwestern China. The giant panda is protected by law.

Mao Zedong (1893-1976) led the struggle to make China a Communist country. From 1949 he was a powerful ruler whose writings influenced many people around the world. After his death, China's leaders began a series of reforms.

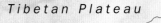

Altay

• Yining

Tian Shan

Urümqi

• Aksu

• Kashi

Taklimakan Desert

C H

• Hotan

Altun Mts

Kunlun Mts

Tibetan Plateau

Himalayas

Lhasa

Everest
29,029ft (8,848m)

0		500 miles
0		500 kilometers

Guilin in southeastern China has some spectacular scenery. Natural crags of limestone rock rise above green rice fields. The rocks have sometimes been likened to dragons' teeth. In Chinese mythology, dragons are friendly not fearsome creatures.

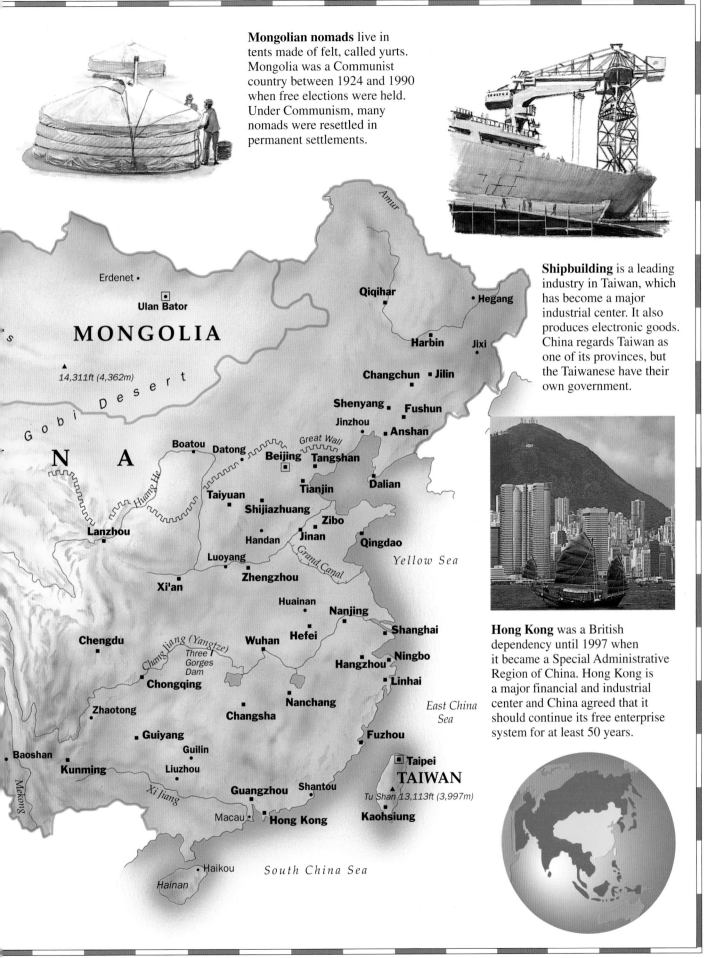

Mongolian nomads live in tents made of felt, called yurts. Mongolia was a Communist country between 1924 and 1990 when free elections were held. Under Communism, many nomads were resettled in permanent settlements.

Shipbuilding is a leading industry in Taiwan, which has become a major industrial center. It also produces electronic goods. China regards Taiwan as one of its provinces, but the Taiwanese have their own government.

Hong Kong was a British dependency until 1997 when it became a Special Administrative Region of China. Hong Kong is a major financial and industrial center and China agreed that it should continue its free enterprise system for at least 50 years.

Erdenet •

⊡ Ulan Bator

MONGOLIA

▲ 14,311ft (4,362m)

Gobi Desert

N   A

Qiqihar

• Hegang

Harbin   Jixi

Changchun • Jilin

Shenyang   • Fushun
Jinzhou
Boatou   Datong   Great Wall   ■ Anshan
               Beijing Tangshan
Huang He   ■ Dalian
         ⊡
Taiyuan ■ Tianjin
  ■ Shijiazhuang
Lanzhou   ■ Zibo
      Handan Jinan
      Luoyang Grand Canal Qingdao
                            Yellow Sea
        ■ Zhengzhou
Xi'an

Huainan
         Nanjing
Chengdu   Hefei
Chang Jiang (Yangtze) Wuhan   ■ Shanghai
Three
Gorges   ■ Ningbo
Dam   Hangzhou
Chongqing   • Linhai
                                East China
         ■ Nanchang   Sea
Zhaotong Changsha
• Guiyang   Fuzhou
    Guilin
Baoshan   Liuzhou   ⊡ Taipei
Kunming   TAIWAN
     Xi Jiang Shantou Tu Shan 13,113ft (3,997m)
        Guangzhou
Macau ■ Hong Kong Kaohsiung
Mekong

• Haikou   South China Sea
Hainan

21

KOREAN PENINSULA

The Korean peninsula juts out from northeastern China, separating the Yellow Sea to the west from the Sea of Japan to the east. From 1910 the Korean peninsula was a Japanese colony. But in 1945, at the end of World War II, Russian troops occupied the northern part of the peninsula, while American forces occupied the south.

This division led to the creation of Communist North Korea and non-Communist South Korea. The two countries fought against each other between 1950 and 1953, when the present boundary was agreed. Tension between them continued throughout the second half of the 20th century. North Korea is less developed than South Korea, which is a fast-growing industrial country.

Kim Il Sung (1912-94) headed the government of North Korea, ruling as a dictator from 1948, when the Communist Democratic People's Republic was established, until his death in 1994. He was succeeded by his son, Kim Jong Il.

 **SOUTH KOREA**

Area: 38,330sq miles (99,274sq km)
Highest point: Halla 6,398ft (1,950m)
Population: 48,847,000
Capital and largest city: Seoul (pop 9,714,000)
Other large cities: Pusan (3,673,000)
Taegu (2,580,000)
Inchon (2,618,000)
Taejon (1,495,000)
Official language: Korean
Religions: Christianity (26%), Buddhism (26%)
Government: Republic
Currency: South Korean won

 **NORTH KOREA**

Area: 46,540sq miles (120,538sq km)
Highest point: Paektu 9,003ft (2,744m)
Population: 23,113,000
Capital and largest city: Pyongyang
(pop 3,228,000)
Other large cities: Hamhung (565,000)
Nampo (455,000)
Chongjin (327,000)
Official language: Korean
Religions: Traditional beliefs, Chondogyo
Government: People's republic
Currency: North Korean won

Seoul, the capital of South Korea, is one of the world's largest cities. Modern skyscrapers show just how fast South Korea has developed since the 1950s. But the city still has many beautiful old buildings.

NORT

Sinuiju

Anju

Taedong

Pyongyang

Nampo

Haeju

Kaeso

Incho

Yellow Sea

0   100 miles

0   100 kilometers

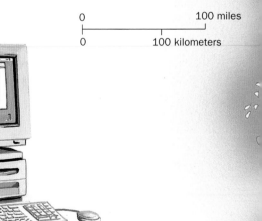

Cars and computers are among the many goods exported by South Korea. The country also ranks among the world's top ten producers of cement, commercial vehicles, steel, televisions and tires.

Che

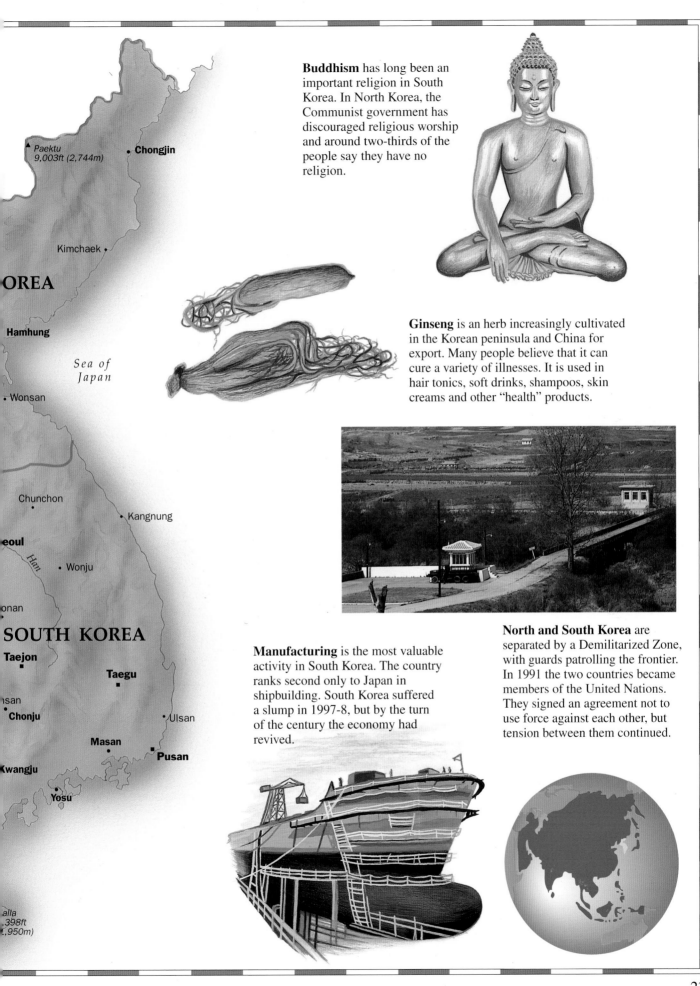

Buddhism has long been an important religion in South Korea. In North Korea, the Communist government has discouraged religious worship and around two-thirds of the people say they have no religion.

Ginseng is an herb increasingly cultivated in the Korean peninsula and China for export. Many people believe that it can cure a variety of illnesses. It is used in hair tonics, soft drinks, shampoos, skin creams and other "health" products.

Manufacturing is the most valuable activity in South Korea. The country ranks second only to Japan in shipbuilding. South Korea suffered a slump in 1997-8, but by the turn of the century the economy had revived.

North and South Korea are separated by a Demilitarized Zone, with guards patrolling the frontier. In 1991 the two countries became members of the United Nations. They signed an agreement not to use force against each other, but tension between them continued.

Paektu
9,003ft (2,744m) •Chongjin

Kimchaek •

OREA

Hamhung

*Sea of
Japan*

•Wonsan

Chunchon
•

•Kangnung

eoul

Han •Wonju

onan

SOUTH KOREA

Taejon

Taegu

san
•**Chonju** •Ulsan

Masan

Kwangju •**Pusan**

•**Yosu**

alla
398ft
,950m)

JAPAN

Japan consists of four large islands, which together make up 98 percent of the country, and thousands of tiny islands. Much of the land is mountainous, but most people live on the small, fertile plains around the coast. Japan lies on an unstable part of the earth, called the Pacific "ring of fire." The country has more than 150 volcanoes, 60 of which are active, and earthquakes are common.

In 1945, after its defeat in World War II, Japan was in ruins. But it is now the world's second biggest economy after the United States. It imports most of the fuels and materials it needs for its huge industries, which have been successful largely through the hard work and skill of its workers and the use of modern technology.

Sumo is a Japanese form of wrestling in which the wrestler tries to throw his opponent to the ground or force him outside a 15-ft (4.6-meter) circle. Judo, karate and kendo (a form of fencing) are other popular sports in Japan.

 **JAPAN**

Area: 145,870sq miles (377,801sq km)
Highest point: Mount Fuji 12,388ft (3,776m)
Population: 127,464,000
Capital and largest city: Tokyo (pop 34,497,000)
Other large cities: Yokohama (3,604,000)
Osaka (2,590,000)
Nagoya (2,195,000)
Sapporo (1,896,000)
Kobe (1,535,000)
Kyoto (1,458,000)
Official language: Japanese
Religions: Shinto and related religions, including Buddhism (84%)
Government: Monarchy
Currency: Yen

Silkworms are the caterpillars, or larvae, of a moth. They feed on the leaves of the white mulberry tree. When fully grown, the silkworms spin a silken cocoon (outer wrapping) around themselves, which is the source of silk thread. Japan is one of the world's top silk producers.

Emperor Akihito is Japan's head of state. He succeeded his father Hirohito in 1989. Before World War II, the Japanese regarded Hirohito as a god. After the war, new laws made him a constitutional monarch.

Mount Fuji is a dormant (sleeping) volcano that last erupted in 1707-8. The snow-capped mountain is on the island of Honshu. The Japanese regard it as a sacred mountain.

Matsue

Okayam
Hiroshima

Inland Sea

Kitakyushu
Tokushir

Matsuyama   Kochi
Fukuoka

Shikoku

Kumamoto
Nagasaki

Kyushu

Miyazaki

Kagoshima

PACIFIC OCEAN

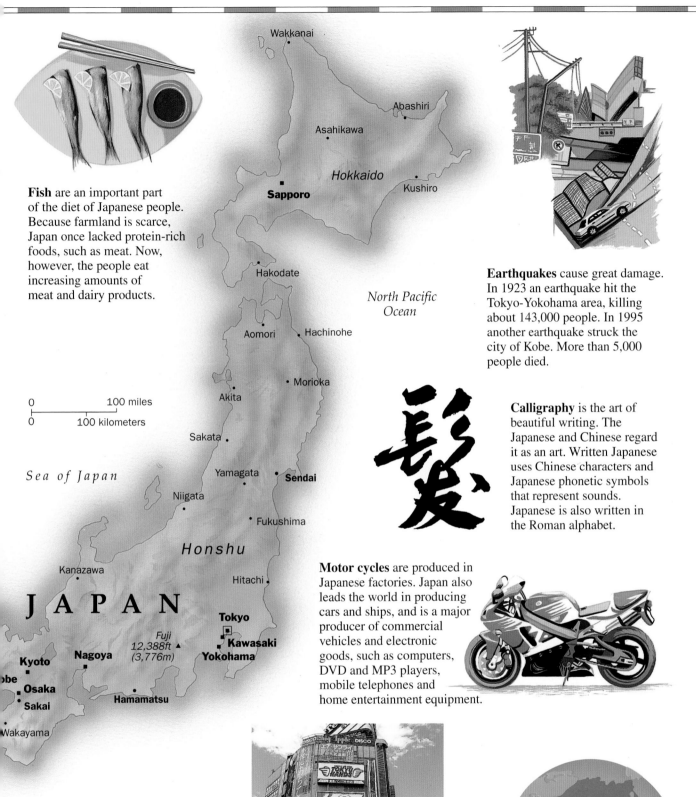

Fish are an important part of the diet of Japanese people. Because farmland is scarce, Japan once lacked protein-rich foods, such as meat. Now, however, the people eat increasing amounts of meat and dairy products.

Wakkanai

Abashiri

Asahikawa

Hokkaido

Sapporo

Kushiro

Hakodate

North Pacific Ocean

Earthquakes cause great damage. In 1923 an earthquake hit the Tokyo-Yokohama area, killing about 143,000 people. In 1995 another earthquake struck the city of Kobe. More than 5,000 people died.

Aomori • Hachinohe

| 0 | 100 miles |
| 0 | 100 kilometers |

• Morioka

Akita

Sakata •

Yamagata • **Sendai**

Niigata •

Calligraphy is the art of beautiful writing. The Japanese and Chinese regard it as an art. Written Japanese uses Chinese characters and Japanese phonetic symbols that represent sounds. Japanese is also written in the Roman alphabet.

• Fukushima

Sea of Japan

Honshu

Kanazawa •

Hitachi •

J A P A N

Fuji 12,388ft ▲ (3,776m)

Tokyo

Kawasaki

Yokohama

Kyoto **Nagoya**

be

Osaka

Sakai **Hamamatsu**

Wakayama

Motor cycles are produced in Japanese factories. Japan also leads the world in producing cars and ships, and is a major producer of commercial vehicles and electronic goods, such as computers, DVD and MP3 players, mobile telephones and home entertainment equipment.

Tokyo, the capital of Japan, is one of the world's largest cities. Its tall buildings and busy streets reflect its importance as Japan's chief business center. But its parks, with their cherry trees, recall traditional Japan.

BANGLADESH, MYANMAR AND THAILAND

Bangladesh was once part of British India. In 1947 it became part of Pakistan and was called East Pakistan. In 1971 East Pakistan broke away and became the independent country of Bangladesh. Bangladesh is a poor but thickly populated country. It is often hit by floods, which cause great human suffering.

Myanmar (formerly Burma) and Thailand are two of the countries in a region called Southeast Asia. Myanmar is another poor country that has been ruled by the military since 1962. Many people have criticized Myanmar's government for its bad human rights record. By contrast, in the second half of the 20th century, Thailand had become one of the wealthier countries in eastern Asia.

An earthquake in the Indian Ocean in 2004 caused a tsunami that devastated Thailand's coast and killed many people.

BANGLADESH

Area: 55,598sq miles (143,998sq km)
Highest point: Mt Keokradong 4,034ft (1,230m)
Population: 147,365,000
Capital and largest city: Dhaka (pop 11,560,000)
Other large cities: Chittagong (3,271,000)
Official language: Bengali
Religions: Islam (83%), Hinduism (16%)
Government: Republic
Currency: Taka

MYANMAR

Area: 261,228sq miles (676,578sq km)
Highest point: Hkakabo Razi 19,296ft (5,881m)
Population: 47,382,000
Capital and largest city: Yangon (pop 3,874,000)
Other large cities: Mandalay (1,237,000)
Official language: Burmese
Religions: Buddhism (89%), Christianity (5%), Islam (4%)
Government: Military regime
Currency: Kyat

THAILAND

Area: 198,115sq miles (513,115sq km)
Highest point: Inthanon Mountain 2,595m (8,514ft)
Population: 64,632,000
Capital and largest city: Bangkok (pop 6,486,000)
Official language: Thai
Religions: Buddhism (95%), Islam (4%)
Government: Monarchy
Currency: Baht

Floods are caused in Bangladesh when heavy rains make the rivers overflow. Other floods occur when tropical storms, called cyclones, hit the coast. Strong winds push seawater inland, flooding the flat coastal plains. Severe flooding was caused by a tsunami that swept the coast of Thailand in 2004.

Buddhist monks are a familiar sight in Myanmar and Thailand. In Myanmar most boys spend time in their local monastery. Some stay for a few weeks, others for years.

Saidpur
Brahmaputra
Mymensingh
Rajshahi
BANGLADESH
Ganges
■ **Dhaka**
• Narayanganj
Khulna
Chittagong
Keokradong
4,034ft (1,230m)
Manda
Sittwe
Bay of Bengal
Irrawaddy
• Pro
INDIAN OCEAN
Yangor
Pathen

0		200 miles
0		200 kilometers

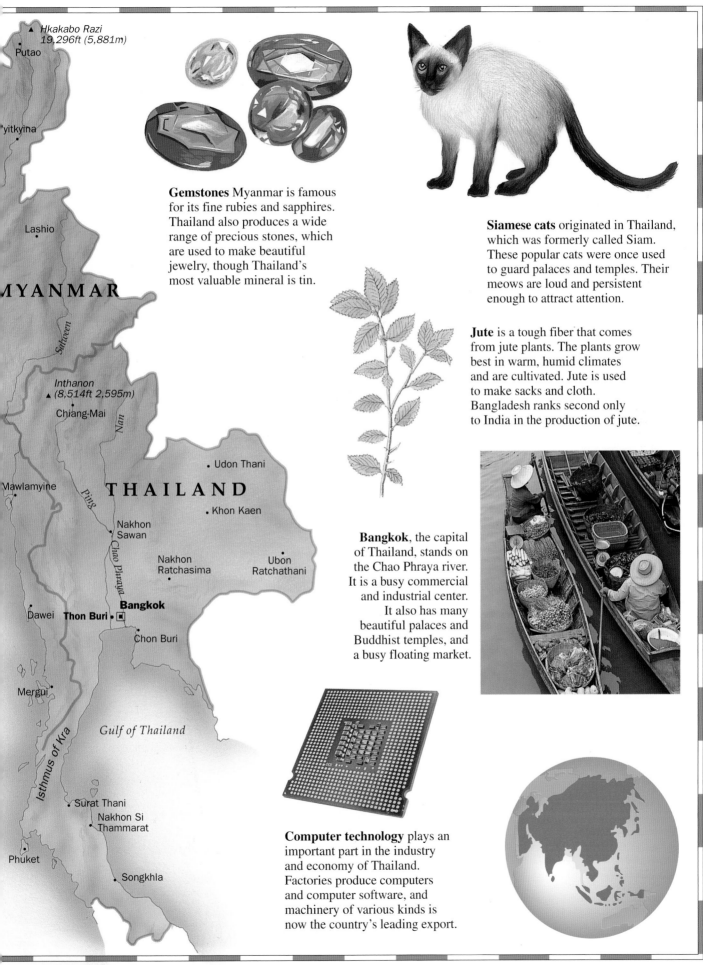

Hkakabo Razi
19,296ft (5,881m)

Putao

'yitkyina

Lashio

MYANMAR

Saluveen

Inthanon
(8,514ft 2,595m)

Chiang-Mai

Nan

Mawlamyine

Ping

THAILAND

Udon Thani

Nakhon
Sawan

Khon Kaen

Chao Phraya

Nakhon
Ratchasima

Ubon
Ratchathani

Dawei   Thon Buri   Bangkok

Chon Buri

Mergui

Gulf of Thailand

Isthmus of Kra

Surat Thani

Nakhon Si
Thammarat

Phuket

Songkhla

Gemstones Myanmar is famous for its fine rubies and sapphires. Thailand also produces a wide range of precious stones, which are used to make beautiful jewelry, though Thailand's most valuable mineral is tin.

Siamese cats originated in Thailand, which was formerly called Siam. These popular cats were once used to guard palaces and temples. Their meows are loud and persistent enough to attract attention.

Jute is a tough fiber that comes from jute plants. The plants grow best in warm, humid climates and are cultivated. Jute is used to make sacks and cloth. Bangladesh ranks second only to India in the production of jute.

Bangkok, the capital of Thailand, stands on the Chao Phraya river. It is a busy commercial and industrial center. It also has many beautiful palaces and Buddhist temples, and a busy floating market.

Computer technology plays an important part in the industry and economy of Thailand. Factories produce computers and computer software, and machinery of various kinds is now the country's leading export.

CAMBODIA, LAOS AND VIETNAM

Cambodia, Laos and Vietnam form a region called Indochina. The region was ruled by France until 1954. Vietnam was divided into two parts: Communist North Vietnam and non-Communist South Vietnam. The division of Vietnam led to the Vietnam War (1957-75). Eventually, Vietnam was reunited as a single Communist country called the Socialist Republic of Vietnam.

Cambodia, Laos and Vietnam are poor developing countries that have been badly scarred by war. Most of their people depend on farming for their living. Manufacturing is increasing, especially in Vietnam.

 **CAMBODIA**

Area: 69,898sq miles (181,035sq km)
Highest point: 5,948ft (1,813m) in west-central Cambodia
Population: 13,881,000
Capital and largest city: Phnom Penh (pop 1,157,000)
Official language: Khmer
Religions: Buddhism (95%)
Government: Republic
Currency: Riel

 **LAOS**

Area: 91,429sq miles (236,800sq km)
Highest point: Mt Bia 9,242ft (2,817m)
Population: 6,368,000
Capital and largest city: Vientiane (pop 716,000)
Other large cities: Pakse (94,000) Savannakhet (68,000)
Official language: Lao
Religions: Buddhism (60%), local religions
Government: People's republic
Currency: Kip

 **VIETNAM**

Area: 128,066sq miles (331,689sq km)
Highest point: Fan Si Pan 10,312ft (3,143m)
Population: 84,403,000
Capital: Hanoi (pop 3,977,000)
Largest cities: Ho Chi Minh City (3,497,000) Haiphong (612,000)
Official language: Vietnamese
Religions: Buddhism (10%), Christianity (9%)
Government: Socialist republic
Currency: Dong

Angkor Wat is a huge temple built in northern Cambodia in the 12th century in honor of the Hindu god Vishnu. It is perhaps the finest of the many ancient temples found in Cambodia.

Rice is the main food crop in all of the three countries in Indochina. The rice shoots are planted in the muddy soil in flooded fields. Rice grows well in the warm, humid climates of these countries.

Lao Ca
Fan Si
10,312ft (

Luang Prabang

LAOS

Mekong

Bia ▲
9,242ft (2,817m

Vientiane

0   100 miles
0   100 kilometers

Sisophon   Angk

Battambang

Lake
Tonle Sa

5,948ft

Gulf of Thailand

Houses in Indochinese villages are often made of wood or bamboo and built on stilts. This keeps them dry when floods occur. About 80 percent of the people of Indochina live in the countryside.

Durian is a fruit grown in Southeast Asia. The spherical fruit has a hard shell. The flesh has a pleasant sweet taste, but the fruit has a strong smell, like ripe cheese.

Mekong River
The Mekong, the longest river in Indochina, rises in Tibet. It forms part of the border between Thailand and Laos and then flows across Laos, Cambodia and Vietnam before emptying into the South China Sea near Ho Chi Minh City.

Ho Chi Minh (1890-1969) was a Vietnamese Communist, who led his country in the struggle for independence from France. He later served as president of Communist North Vietnam during the Vietnam War.

Ha Giang

Lang Son •

Hanoi
◘

Hoa Binh • • **Haiphong**

Ninh Binh

VIETNAM

• Vinh

South China Sea

Savannakhet

Annamite Range

Mekong

Quang Tri
Hue

• **Da Nang**

• Pakse

• Qui Nhon

• Stung Treng

CAMBODIA

Kompong
Cham

Da Lat

• Nha Trang

Cam Ranh

nom Penh • Tay Ninh

Mekong

■ **Ho Chi Minh City**

• My Tho

ach Gia •

Can Tho

Ca Mau

MALAYSIA, SINGAPORE AND BRUNEI

Malaysia is a large country. It includes the Malaysian peninsula, which is joined to mainland Asia, and two areas in northern Borneo called Sabah and Sarawak. This hot and rainy country has developed quickly since 1963, when Malaya, a British territory until 1957, agreed to unite with Singapore, Sabah and Sarawak.

Singapore, a small island country that was also once ruled by Britain, withdrew from Malaysia in 1965. It is now one of the most prosperous places in Asia. Brunei, a small country in Borneo, which became independent from Britain in 1984, is also prosperous. Its wealth comes from its rich oil reserves.

Singapore consists of one large island, also called Singapore, and 58 small ones. Its people are highly skilled and hardworking, and have made their country a major industrial center. Trade and finance are also important.

MALAYSIA

Area: 127,320sq miles (329,758sq km)
Highest point: Mt Kinabalu 13,431ft (4,094m)
Population: 24,386,000
Capital and largest city: Kuala Lumpur (pop 1,352,000)
Other large cities: Johor Baharu (839,000) Ipoh (692,000)
Official language: Malay
Religions: Islam (53%), Buddhism (17%)
Government: Federal monarchy
Currency: Ringgit

SINGAPORE

Area: 239sq miles (618sq km)
Population: 4,492,000
Capital: Singapore (pop 4,253,000)
Official languages: Chinese, English, Malay, Tamil
Religions: Buddhism (43%), Islam (15%), Taoism (9%)
Government: Republic
Currency: Singaporean dollar

BRUNEI

Area: 2,226sq miles (5,765sq km)
Population: 379,000
Capital: Bandar Seri Begawan (pop 61,000)
Official language: Malay
Religions: Islam (67%), Buddhism (13%), Christianity (10%)
Government: Monarchy
Currency: Bruneian dollar

Alor Setar

Kota Baharu

George Town

Kuala Terengganu

Ipoh

Cameron Highlands

MALAYSIA

Kuantan

Kuala Lumpur

Kelang

Straits of Malacca

Seremban

Keluang

Melaka

Johor Baharu

Singapore

SINGAPORE

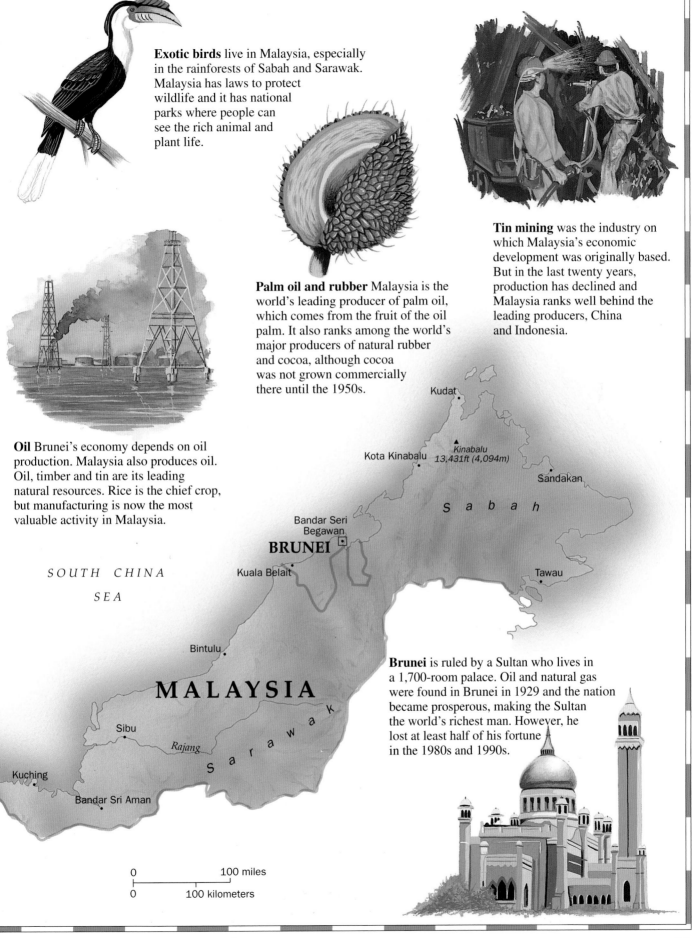

Exotic birds live in Malaysia, especially in the rainforests of Sabah and Sarawak. Malaysia has laws to protect wildlife and it has national parks where people can see the rich animal and plant life.

Palm oil and rubber Malaysia is the world's leading producer of palm oil, which comes from the fruit of the oil palm. It also ranks among the world's major producers of natural rubber and cocoa, although cocoa was not grown commercially there until the 1950s.

Tin mining was the industry on which Malaysia's economic development was originally based. But in the last twenty years, production has declined and Malaysia ranks well behind the leading producers, China and Indonesia.

Oil Brunei's economy depends on oil production. Malaysia also produces oil. Oil, timber and tin are its leading natural resources. Rice is the chief crop, but manufacturing is now the most valuable activity in Malaysia.

Brunei is ruled by a Sultan who lives in a 1,700-room palace. Oil and natural gas were found in Brunei in 1929 and the nation became prosperous, making the Sultan the world's richest man. However, he lost at least half of his fortune in the 1980s and 1990s.

Kudat

Kota Kinabalu ▲ *Kinabalu* 13,431ft (4,094m)

Sandakan

S a b a h

Bandar Seri Begawan

BRUNEI

Kuala Belait

Tawau

SOUTH CHINA

SEA

Bintulu

MALAYSIA

Sibu

Rajang

S a r a w a k

Kuching

Bandar Sri Aman

0   100 miles

0   100 kilometers

INDONESIA AND EAST TIMOR

A mainly Muslim country, Indonesia is made up of about 13,600 islands, though fewer than 6,000 are inhabited. Most of the islands are mountainous and many mountains are active volcanoes. The bigger islands also have large coastal lowlands. The country has a hot and wet climate, with large rainforests.

Indonesia became independent from the Netherlands in 1949, but Portugal continued to rule the eastern part of the island of Timor until 1975. Indonesia ruled the area from 1976 until 1999, when the local people voted to make East Timor an independent country. It became independent in 2002.

Orangutans are large apes that live in the forests of Borneo and Sumatra. They have recently been threatened by forest clearance and huge forest fires.

INDONESIA

Area: 735,358sq miles (1,904,569sq km)
Highest point: Puncak Jaya 16,503ft (5,030m)
Population: 245,453,000
Capital and largest city: Jakarta
(pop 12,296,000)
Other large cities: Surabaya (2,367,000)
Medan (1,758,000)
Bandung (1,676,000)
Bekasi (1,569,000)
Palembang (1,250,000)
Official language: Bahasa Indonesia
Religions: Islam (88%), Christianity (8%)
Government: Republic
Currency: Indonesian rupiah

Tourism is an important activity in Indonesia. The island of Bali, with its beautiful beaches, its ancient Hindu culture and attractions such as classical dancing, is particularly popular. But tourism has been hit since 2002 by bombings in tourist areas.

Krakatoa was one of the many volcanic islands in Indonesia. In 1883 it exploded with great force. The explosion triggered a destructive wave called a tsunami which drowned 36,000 people on nearby Sumatra and Java. About two-thirds of the island disappeared.

Tsunami In December 2004, an undersea earthquake off the coast of Sumatra near Banda Aceh triggered a tsunami that struck the coast of Indonesia and other countries. It wiped out whole communities, killing more than 200,000 people in the region and making many more homeless.

Spices are an important crop in Indonesia. Rice is the chief food crop and coffee, palm oil, rubber, sugar cane, tea and tobacco are exported. Agriculture employs about 40 percent of the work force.

EAST TIMOR

Area: 5,641sq miles (14,609sq km)
Highest point: Foto Tatamailau 9,721ft (2,963m)
Population: 1,063,000
Capital and largest city: Dili (49,000)
Official languages: Tetum, Portuguese
Religions: Roman Catholic (90%) Islam (4%)
Government: Republic
Currency: US dollar

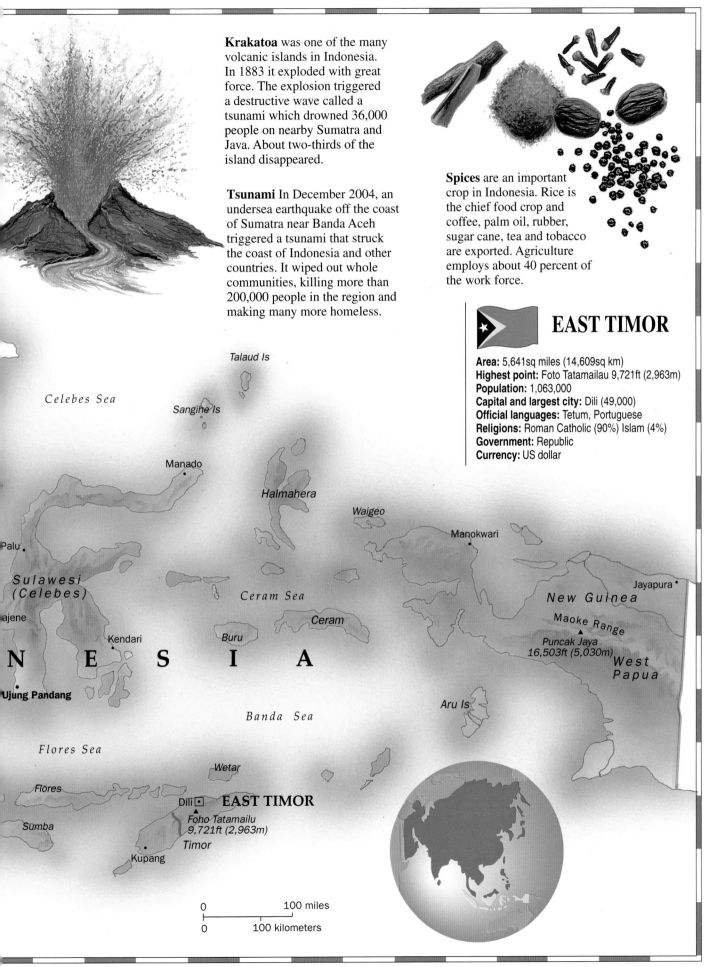

Talaud Is

Celebes Sea

Sangihe Is

Manado

Halmahera

Waigeo

Manokwari

Palu

Sulawesi
(Celebes)

Ceram Sea

Ceram

New Guinea

Maoke Range

Puncak Jaya
16,503ft (5,030m)

West
Papua

Jayapura

ajene

Kendari

Buru

N E S I A

Ujung Pandang

Aru Is

Banda Sea

Flores Sea

Wetar

Flores

Dili ▣ **EAST TIMOR**

Sumba

▲ Foho Tatamailu
9,721ft (2,963m)

Timor

Kupang

| 0 | 100 miles |
| 0 | 100 kilometers |

PHILIPPINES

The Philippines consists of about 7,100 islands, about 1,000 of which are inhabited. The country lies in the Pacific "ring of fire," so volcanic eruptions and earthquakes are common. Much of the land is mountainous. Agriculture employs about 35 percent of the country's workers, and bananas, cocoa, coconuts, coffee, corn, rice (the staple food), sugar cane and tobacco are leading crops. Manufacturing is increasing.

Spain ruled the Philippines from 1565 until 1898, when the United States took over. Japan invaded the Philippines during World War II, but the country became fully independent in 1946.

PHILIPPINES

Area: 115,830sq miles (300,000sq km)
Highest point: Mount Apo 9,692ft (2,954m)
Population: 89,469,000
Capital: Manila (pop 10,352,000)
Other large cities: Quezon City (2,174,000)
Davao (1,245,000)
Caloocan (1,178,000)
Cebu (719,000)
Official languages: Filipino, English
Religions: Christianity (Roman Catholic 81%, Protestant 10%), Islam 5%
Government: Republic
Currency: Philippine peso

Christianity Spain claimed the Philippines in 1565 and missionaries soon began to convert the people to Christianity. As a result, the Philippines has more Christians than any other Asian country. Here Roman Catholics gather for an open-air Communion rally.

Forests cover about one-third of the land in the Philippines. Some hardwood trees known as Philippine mahoganies provide valuable timber. The country also produces bamboo and kapok, a fiber used in upholstery.

Map labels

South China Sea
Laoag
Apa
Luzon
Cagayan
Dagupan
PHILIPPINES
Tarlac
Angeles
Caloocan
Olongapo
Quezon
Manila
San Pa
Batangas
Mindoro
Puerto Princesa
Palawan
Sulu Sea
Balabac
0   100 miles
0   100 kilometers
Zamboa
Basila
Jolo
Tawi-Tawi

Ferdinand Marcos (1917-89) was president of the Philippines from 1965 until 1986. Accused of corruption and election fraud, he fled the country in 1986. The Philippines faces several political problems including conflict with Muslim guerrillas, crime and unemployment.

Jeepneys are a popular means of transport in the Philippines. These highly decorated shared taxis provide cheap transport for their passengers, who are crammed in. Buses are also important.

PACIFIC OCEAN

Catanduanes

• Naga

▲ Mayon Volcano
2421m

Masbate

Samar

anay

• Tacloban

ilo

Cebu *Leyte*

• Bacolod

Dinagat

• **Cebu**

Siargao

egros *Bohol*

• Butuan

• Dipolog

• Cagayan de Oro

Mindanao

• Pagadian

Datu Piang

▲ **Davao**

Apo
9,692ft (2,954m)

General Santos

Manila, the capital of the Philippines, is also the country's chief commercial and cultural center, as well as being the main port. It is a beautiful city on the shores of Manila Bay on Luzon island, but it has many slums where people live in desperate poverty.

Philippine eagles are also called monkey-eating eagles. They are found only in the Philippines. These eagles eat not just monkeys but also other mammals, birds and reptiles. They are becoming scarce because the rainforest trees in which they nest are being cut down.

Sugar cane grows well in the fertile, volcanic soils of the Philippines. Sugar cane is a plant that belongs to the grass family. Its stalks contain a sweet juice from which sugar and syrup are made.

PEOPLE AND BELIEFS

More than 60 percent of the world's people live in Asia. Vast areas are too dry, too cold or too mountainous for people to live in them. By contrast, some parts of eastern, southeastern and southern Asia are among the most densely populated places in the world. Many people live in huge cities. Asia's largest cities include Tokyo (Japan), Jakarta (Indonesia), Seoul (South Korea), Mumbai, (India), Shanghai (China) and Delhi (India).

The Dome of the Rock mosque rises above the Wailing Wall in Jerusalem. Islam, Hinduism and Buddhism are the main faiths in Asia. There are fewer than five million Jews.

Population densities in Asia

Number of people
per square kilometer*

- Over 100
- Between 50 and 100
- Between 10 and 50
- Between 1 and 10
- Below 1

■ Cities of more than 1,000,000 people

● Cities of more than 500,000 people

* 1 square kilometer = .4 square mile

Population and area

Although only 75 percent of Russia lies in Asia, it is Asia's largest country. The next largest countries in Asia are China, India, Kazakhstan (a small proportion of which is in Europe), Saudi Arabia and the island country of Indonesia.

China and India have more people than any other countries in the world. Indonesia ranks fourth, after the United States. Russia ranks sixth in population, but about 80 percent of Russia's population lives in European Russia. Pakistan, Bangladesh and Japan also have huge populations.

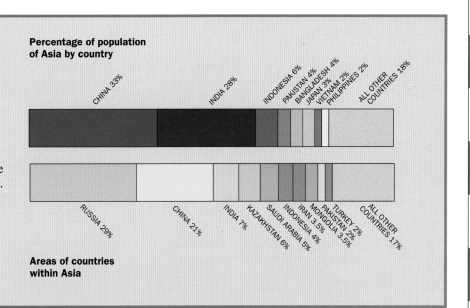

Percentage of population of Asia by country

CHINA 33% · INDIA 28% · INDONESIA 6% · PAKISTAN 4% · BANGLADESH 4% · JAPAN 3% · VIETNAM 2% · PHILIPPINES 2% · ALL OTHER COUNTRIES 18%

RUSSIA 29% · CHINA 21% · INDIA 7% · KAZAKHSTAN 6% · SAUDI ARABIA 5% · INDONESIA 4% · IRAN 3.5% · MONGOLIA 3.5% · PAKISTAN 2% · TURKEY 2% · ALL OTHER COUNTRIES 17%

Areas of countries within Asia

Main religions

All the world's major religions were founded in Asia. Judaism, Christianity and Islam all began in southwestern Asia. Today, most people in southwestern Asia are Muslims, but Judaism is the chief religion in Israel and Christianity the chief religion in Cyprus. Hinduism began in India and, today, more than four-fifths of the people of India are Hindus. But Muslims make up about 13 percent of the people of India, while Islam is also the chief religion in Bangladesh, the Maldives and Pakistan.

Buddhism, which began in India about 2,500 years ago, has spread into much of eastern Asia. Islam is the chief religion of Brunei, Indonesia and Malaysia, while Christianity is the main religion in the Philippines. Some local religions survive in remote areas in Indonesia. Confucianism is important in eastern Asia, while Shinto is followed in Japan.

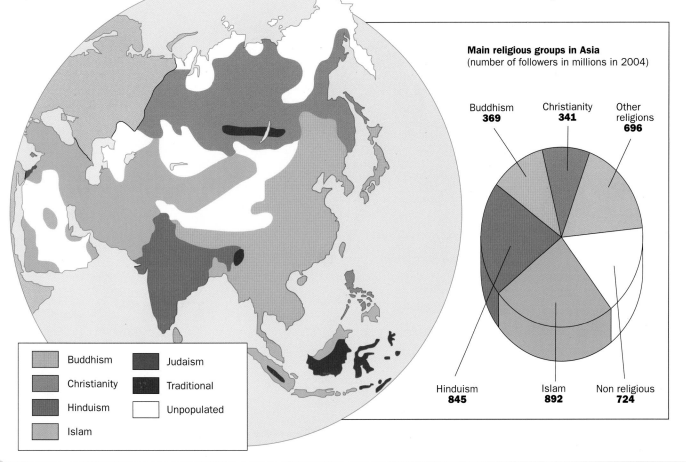

Buddhism
Christianity
Hinduism
Islam
Judaism
Traditional
Unpopulated

Main religious groups in Asia
(number of followers in millions in 2004)

Buddhism **369**
Christianity **341**
Other religions **696**
Hinduism **845**
Islam **892**
Non religious **724**

CLIMATE AND VEGETATION

Asia's climates range from polar and tundra in the north, to hot tropical in the south. South of the polar region, much of Siberia, in northern Asia, has a cold climate, with vast coniferous forests of fir, pine and spruce. In eastern Asia, these forests merge into mixed forest, with tropical forests in the southeast and parts of India. Central Asia has grassy steppe and cold deserts, while hot deserts cover much of southwestern Asia.

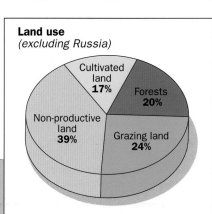

Land use
(excluding Russia)

- Cultivated land **17%**
- Forests **20%**
- Non-productive land **39%**
- Grazing land **24%**

☐ Polar	☐ Steppe (short grass)	
◼ Mountain	☐ Savanna	
◻ Tundra	◼ Tropical rainforest	
◻ Coniferous forest	◻ Monsoon forest	
◻ Mixed forest	◻ Dry tropical forest	
◻ Broadleaf forest	☐ Subtropical forest	
◻ Mediterranean	◻ Dry tropical scrub	
◻ Prairie (long grass)	◻ Desert	

Temperature
key scale in °F (°C)

- Below –26°F (Below –32°C)
- –26 to –11°F (–32 to –24°C)
- –11 to 3°F (–24 to –16°C)
- 3 to 18°F (–16 to –8°C)
- 18 to 32°F (–8 to 0°C)
- 32 to 46°F (0 to 8°C)
- 46 to 61°F (8 to 16°C)
- 61 to 75°F (16 to 24°C)
- 75 to 90°F (24 to 32°C)
- Above 90°F (Above 32°C)

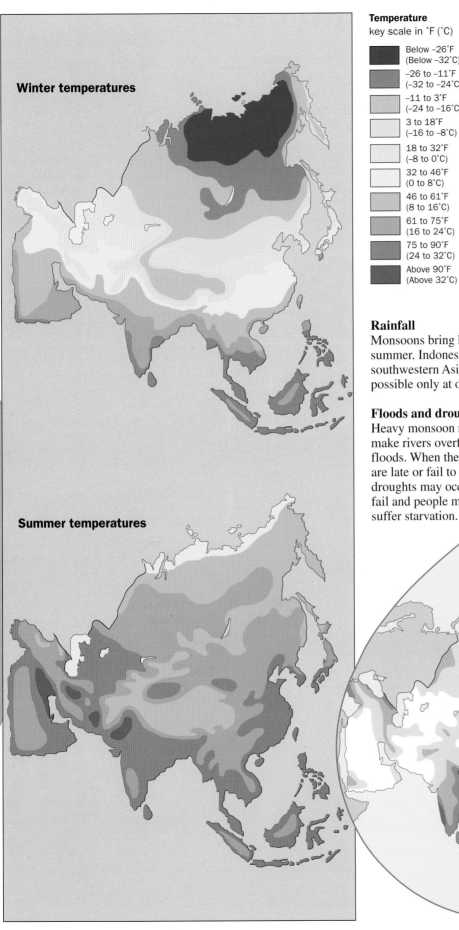

Winter temperatures

Summer temperatures

Range of climates
Temperature and precipitation (rain, snow and all other forms of moisture that come from the air) are the two main factors that determine climate. Asia's climate varies from the Arctic north to the equatorial regions in the southeast. The climate is influenced by the distance a place is from the sea. Extreme climates, with hot summers and bitterly cold winters and little precipitation, occur in central Asia.

In southern Asia, winds blow outwards from the land to the sea in winter. In summer, the land heats up and moist air is drawn inland from the sea. This causes a reversal of wind directions. These seasonal winds are called monsoons.

Rainfall
Monsoons bring heavy rain to India and other areas in summer. Indonesia has rain throughout the year, while southwestern Asia has a hot desert climate. Life is possible only at oases – places where water is available.

Floods and droughts
Heavy monsoon rains sometimes make rivers overflow, causing floods. When the monsoon winds are late or fail to bring enough rain, droughts may occur. Crops fail and people may suffer starvation.

Annual rainfall
in inches (mm)

- Above 118in (3,000mm)
- 79 - 118in (2,000 - 3,000mm)
- 39 - 79in (1,000 - 2,000mm)
- 20 - 39in (500 - 1,000mm)
- 10 - 20in (250 - 500mm)
- 0 - 10in (0 - 250mm)

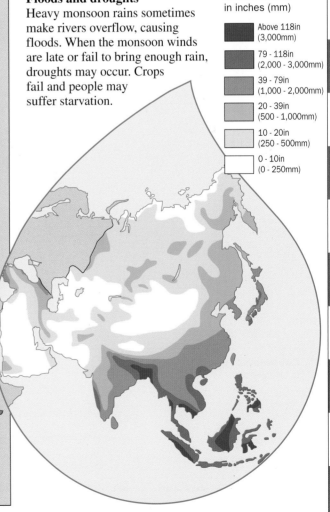

ECOLOGY AND ENVIRONMENT

Currently Asia's population is increasing every year by more than 50 million. Many parts of Asia are overcrowded and, as the population increases, overcrowding grows worse. The yearly increase in population creates pressure on the land, with rainforests being cleared to provide timber and fuel, and land for farming and human settlement. In some areas, the cutting down of trees has led to environmental disasters and a great reduction in the numbers of wild animals and plants. Unknown numbers of plant species, some that might have been of medicinal value, become extinct all the time.

Rice is harvested on land that was once rainforest. The people need the food, but the environmental cost is unknown.

Environmental damage to land and sea

- Existing desert
- Area at risk of desertification
- Present rainforest
- Rainforest seriously damaged in recent years
- Most polluted seas
- Most polluted rivers
- Area most affected by acid rain
- Serious pollution from cities

Damaging the environment

When forests in upland areas are cut down, the effects are felt in the lowlands. Without trees to soak up the water and anchor the soil, the rain flows over the surface, washing away fertile soils. The soil is swept into the swollen rivers, where it piles up on the river beds. This makes the rivers overflow their banks, causing floods. Serious floods occurred in India in 2005.

In the late 1990s, forest fires in Indonesia, many deliberately started to clear the land, caused clouds of smoke that choked people in countries to the north, such as Malaysia and Singapore.

In Asia's overcrowded cities, factories and cars fill the air with gases, causing severe air pollution. Factories also tip harmful chemicals into rivers, making the water poisonous. Human populations use the river water for washing and also for disposing of waste. But the rivers are unable to cope with the amount of pollution and clean water is becoming increasingly scarce.

Natural hazards

Earthquakes occur in a band stretching from Turkey to the Himalayas. Earthquakes and volcanic eruptions are also common in southeastern and eastern Asia, which forms part of the Pacific "ring of fire" where movements between the earth's crustal plates occur. In 2004 an undersea earthquake off the coast of Sumatra created a huge wave, called a tsunami, which flooded coastal areas of 12 Indian Ocean nations and killed more than 200,000 people.

Tropical storms, which drive seawater inland, causing floods, are another hazard facing the poor in southern and southeastern Asia. In 1970, a storm in Bangladesh killed about a million people.

Endangered species

The natural habitats of many animals have been greatly reduced as the human population has increased. Many kinds of animals are now endangered. The most famous example is the giant panda, the symbol of the WWF (formerly World Wide Fund for Nature). It lives in what remains of the cold forests in China's Sichuan province. Most of the trees and bamboos have been cut down by local people to build homes and for firewood.

Many animals, such as tigers and monkeys, are hunted by poachers for their skins and for body parts that are used in folk medicines. Some, including orangutans, are caught as babies and sold as pets. Orangutans have also been threatened by forest clearance and uncontrolled fires. Some species, including the large birdwing butterflies and many rainforest trees, are now protected.

Javan rhinoceros
Some endangered species of Asia

Mammals and reptiles
Asian elephant
Giant panda
Javan and Sumatran rhinos
Orangutan
Snow leopard
Tiger
Komodo dragon
Marine turtles

Birds
Gurney's pitta
Japanese crane
Philippine monkey-eating eagle
Rothschild's mynah

Plants and trees
Blue vanda orchid
Dove tree
Paphiopedilum orchid
Rafflesia arnoldii

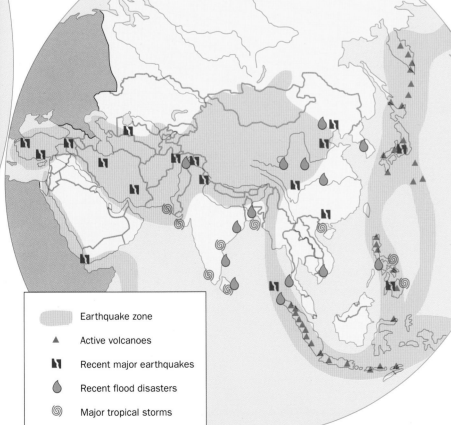

Earthquake zone

▲ Active volcanoes

Recent major earthquakes

Recent flood disasters

Major tropical storms

ECONOMY

More than half the people of Asia make their living by farming. Many farmers are poor and grow little more than they need to feed their families. The use of machinery, fertilizers and new, higher-producing seeds of such crops as rice and wheat, have raised production in recent years. Japan is a major industrial power and manufacturing is increasing, especially in eastern Asia, from Indonesia to Korea.

All over Asia old-fashioned factories are being modernized to cope with increasing trade with the rest of the world.

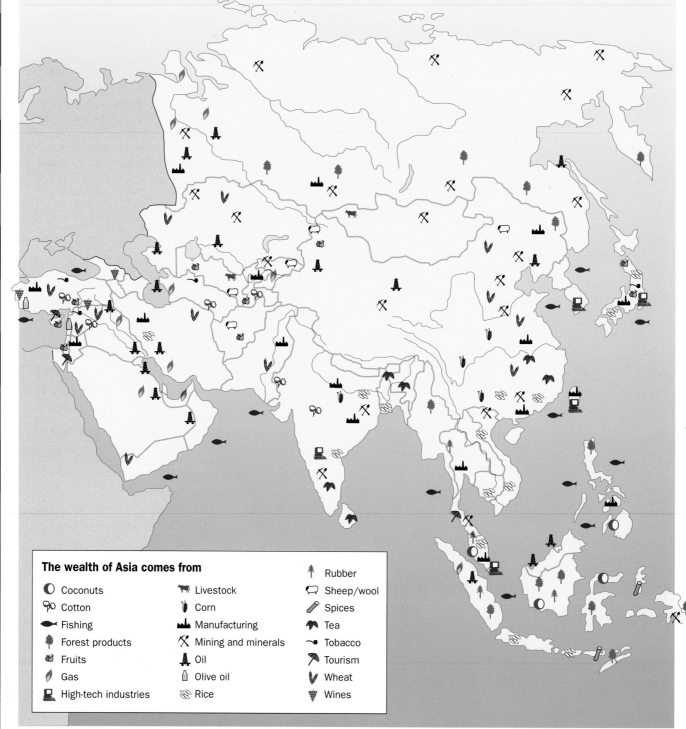

The wealth of Asia comes from

- ☾ Coconuts
- ⚘ Cotton
- 🐟 Fishing
- 🌲 Forest products
- 🍒 Fruits
- 🍃 Gas
- 💻 High-tech industries
- 🐄 Livestock
- 🌽 Corn
- 🏭 Manufacturing
- ⚒ Mining and minerals
- ⛽ Oil
- 🧴 Olive oil
- ❀ Rice
- 🌲 Rubber
- 🐑 Sheep/wool
- 🌶 Spices
- 🌿 Tea
- 🚬 Tobacco
- 🏖 Tourism
- 🌾 Wheat
- 🍇 Wines

Gross domestic product

In order to compare the economies of countries, experts work out the gross domestic product (GDP) of the country in US dollars. The GDP is the total value of the goods and services produced by a country in a year. The chart shows that Japan has the highest GDP. Its GDP ranks second only in the world to that of the United States. It is almost twice that of China and more than five times larger than the GDP of India.

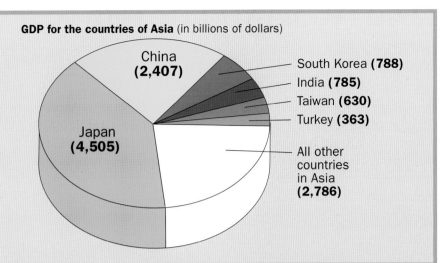

GDP for the countries of Asia (in billions of dollars)

China (2,407)

South Korea (788)
India (785)
Taiwan (630)
Turkey (363)

All other countries in Asia (2,786)

Japan (4,505)

Sources of energy

Several of Asia's leading industrial countries, including Japan, lack oil, natural gas and coal. They have to import these fuels to produce the energy they need. Several Asian countries are, however, major fuel producers. Southwestern Asia is a leading source of oil. Saudi Arabia leads the world in oil production and it contains the largest known reserves. Iran and the United Arab Emirates also ranked among the world's top ten producers in 2005, as did Russia, which now rivals Saudi Arabia. Russia, Iran, Indonesia, Saudi Arabia and Uzbekistan are also major producers of natural gas. China leads the world in coal production, while India, Russia and Kazakhstan are other leading coal producers.

Per capita GDPs

Per capita means per head or per person. Per capita GDPs are worked out by dividing the GDP by the population. Japan has the highest per capita GDP in Asia, but tiny Singapore, with its many industries, also has a high per capita GDP. Countries with low per capita GDPs are Afghanistan, Cambodia, Nepal and Yemen.

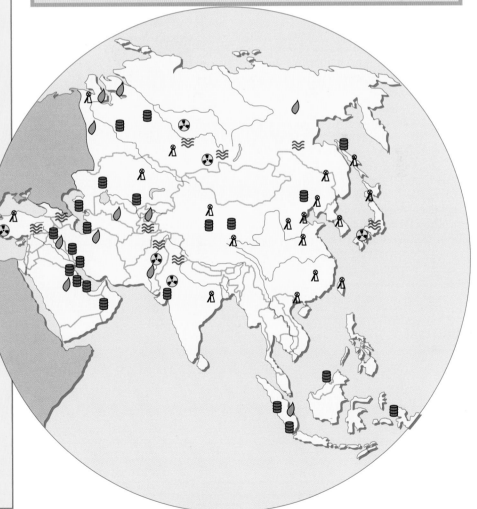

Sources of energy found in Asia

- ▤ Oil
- ◗ Gas
- ≋ Hydroelectricity
- ⚒ Coal
- ☢ Uranium

POLITICS AND HISTORY

The world map is always changing. From the 1940s, country after country in Asia became independent. In 1947 British India was divided into India and Pakistan. These two countries still dispute their boundaries. In 1991 the nations of Kazakhstan, Kyrgyzstan, Tajikistan, Turkmenistan and Uzbekistan were created when the Soviet Union split up. In 1997, British Hong Kong became part of China and, in 2002, East Timor broke away from Indonesia to become an independent nation.

Great events

The oldest known civilizations were founded in Mesopotamia in what is now Iraq. Other great civilizations grew up in the Indus River valley and in China. Asia was also the birthplace of the world's major religions.

Contact with Europe increased rapidly from the early 16th century when the Portuguese found new sea routes from Europe to Asia. Then came Spanish, Dutch and British traders and missionaries. By the 19th century, European powers had colonized much of Asia. In the late 19th and early 20th centuries, Japan emerged as a military power, but it was finally defeated in 1945 when the first atomic bombs were dropped on the country.

In the late 1940s, several Asian countries became independent and, in 1949, a Communist government took over in China. The spread of Communism led to wars in Korea (1950-3) and Vietnam (1954-75). Japan, with help from the United States, recovered to become a major world economic power. From the 1970s, several countries, including Hong Kong (part of China since 1997), South Korea, Singapore, Taiwan and Thailand, and more recently China itself, have built up their economies, but many Asians remain poor.

The 21st century has seen a rise in terrorism resulting in wars in Afghanistan and Iraq. The restoration of peace and the fight against poverty are Asia's main challenges.

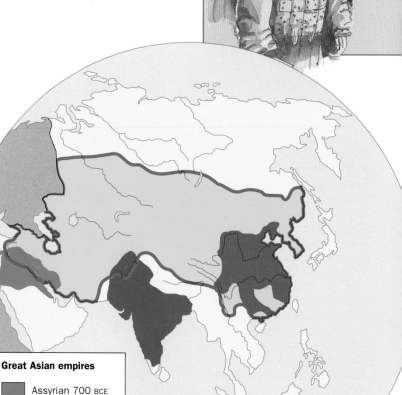

Great Asian empires

- Assyrian 700 BCE
- Ch'in 200 BCE
- Mongol 1300
- Mughal 1700

Important dates

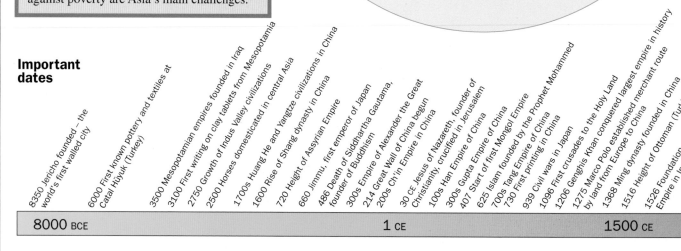

8350 Jericho founded – the world's first walled city

6000 First known pottery and textiles at Catal Hüyük (Turkey)

3500 Mesopotamian empires founded in Iraq

3100 First writing on clay tablets from Mesopotamia

2750 Growth of Indus Valley civilizations

2500 Horses domesticated in central Asia

1700s Huang He and Yangtze civilizations in China

1600 Rise of Shang dynasty in China

720 Height of Assyrian Empire

660 Jimmu, first emperor of Japan

486 Death of Siddhartha Gautama, founder of Buddhism

300s Empire of Alexander the Great

214 Great Wall of China begun

200s Ch'in Empire in China

30 CE Jesus of Nazareth, founder of Christianity, crucified in Jerusalem

100s Han Empire of China

300s Gupta Empire of China

407 Start of first Mongol Empire

625 Islam founded by the Prophet Mohammed

700s Tang Empire of China

730 First printing in China

939 Civil wars in Japan

1096 First crusades to the Holy Land

1206 Genghis Khan conquered largest empire in history

1275 Marco Polo established largest merchant route by land from Europe to China

1368 Ming dynasty founded in China

1516 Height of Ottoman (Turkish) Empire

1526 Foundation of Mughal Empire in India

8000 BCE	1 CE	1500 CE

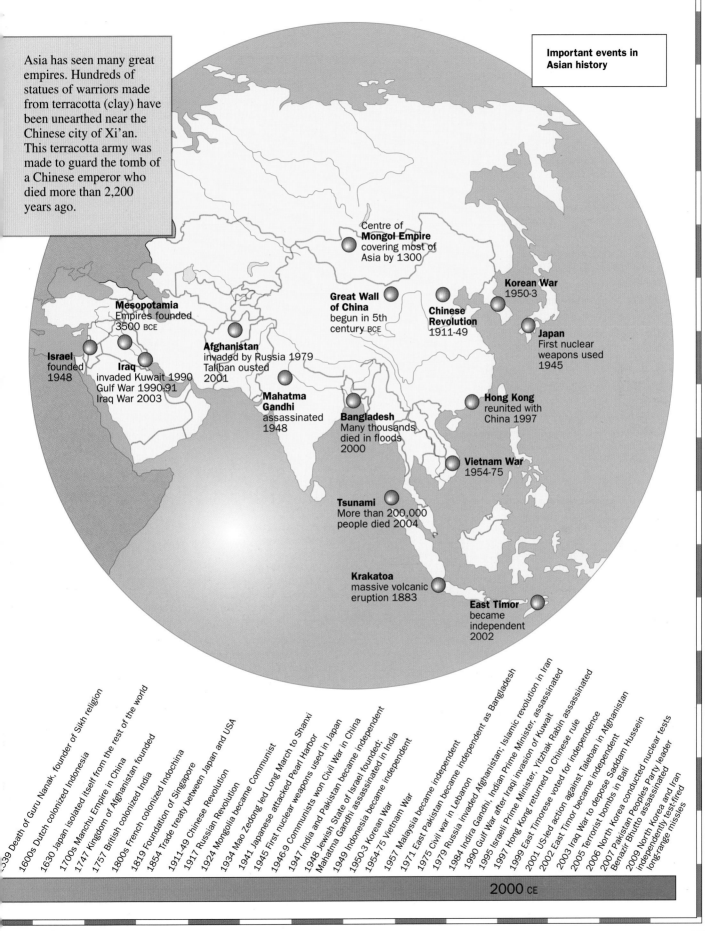

Asia has seen many great empires. Hundreds of statues of warriors made from terracotta (clay) have been unearthed near the Chinese city of Xi'an. This terracotta army was made to guard the tomb of a Chinese emperor who died more than 2,200 years ago.

Centre of **Mongol Empire** covering most of Asia by 1300

Korean War 1950-3

Great Wall of China begun in 5th century BCE

Chinese Revolution 1911-49

Japan First nuclear weapons used 1945

Mesopotamia Empires founded 3500 BCE

Israel founded 1948

Iraq invaded Kuwait 1990 Gulf War 1990-91 Iraq War 2003

Afghanistan invaded by Russia 1979 Taliban ousted 2001

Mahatma Gandhi assassinated 1948

Hong Kong reunited with China 1997

Bangladesh Many thousands died in floods 2000

Vietnam War 1954-75

Tsunami More than 200,000 people died 2004

Krakatoa massive volcanic eruption 1883

East Timor became independent 2002

539 Death of Guru Nanak, founder of Sikh religion
1600s Dutch colonized Indonesia
1630 Japan isolated itself from the rest of the world
1700s Manchu Empire in China
1747 Kingdom of Afghanistan founded
1757 British colonized India
1800s French colonized Indochina
1819 Foundation of Singapore
1854 Trade treaty between Japan and USA
1911-49 Chinese Revolution
1917 Russian Revolution
1924 Mongolia became Communist
1934 Mao Zedong led Long March to Shanxi
1941 Japanese attacked Pearl Harbor
1945 First nuclear weapons used in Japan
1946-9 Communists won Civil War in China
1947 India and Pakistan became independent
1948 Jewish State of Israel founded;
Mahatma Gandhi assassinated in India
1949 Indonesia became independent
1950-3 Korean War
1954-75 Vietnam War
1957 Malaysia became independent
1971 East Pakistan became independent as Bangladesh
1975 Civil war in Lebanon
1979 Russia invaded Afghanistan; Islamic revolution in Iran
1984 Indira Gandhi, Indian Prime Minister, assassinated
1990 Gulf War after Iraqi invasion of Kuwait
1995 Israeli Prime Minister, Yitzhak Rabin assassinated
1997 Hong Kong returned to Chinese rule
1999 East Timorese voted for independence
2001 US-led action against Taleban in Afghanistan
2002 East Timor became independent
2003 Iraq War to depose Saddam Hussein
2005 Terrorist bombs in Bali
2006 North Korea conducted nuclear tests
2007 Pakistan Peoples Party leader Benazir Bhutto assassinated
2009 North Korea and Iran independently test-fired long-range missiles

2000 CE

45

GLOSSARY

Al Qaeda Arabic, meaning "the foundation," Al Qaeda is an independent military organization that is heavily influenced by its interpretation of the Islamic religion. Established by Osama bin Laden in 1988, it is widely regarded as a terrorist organization.

assassinate To kill someone, especially a political leader or other public figure, by a sudden, violent attack.

brutality Cruel, harsh, or ruthless behavior or treatment.

Communion A Christian sacrament in which consecrated bread and wine are consumed as memorials of Christ's death or as symbols of the body and blood of Christ.

Communist A supporter of a political theory or system in which all property and wealth is owned in a classless society by all the member of that society.

constitutional monarchy A political system in which the head of state is a king or queen ruling to the extent allowed by a constitution.

devout Deeply religious; devoted to a particular personal interest or cause.

dictator A powerful ruler; a leader who rules a country with absolute power, usually by force.

dormant Temporarily inactive, or not actively growing.

emirate An area ruled by an emir (who, in some Islamic countries, is an independent ruler, commander, or governor; an emir is also a title for a descendant of the prophet Muhammad).

endangered species Species threatened by extinction; a species whose numbers are so few, or are decreasing so quickly, that the animal, plant, or other organism may soon die out.

export To send goods for sale or exchange to other countries.

extinct No longer in existence; having died out or ceased to exist.

famine A severed shortage of food that results in widespread hunger.

federation A political unit formed from smaller units on a federal basis.

habitat The natural conditions and environment in which a plant or animal lives, such as forest, desert, or wetlands.

hajj The pilgrimage to Mecca, Saudi Arabia, that is a principal religious obligation of adult Muslims.

kando A form of fencing (sword fighting).

monarchy A political system in which a state is ruled by a monarch.

monsoon Seasonal winds; a period of heavy rainfall, especially during the summer over South and Southeast Asia.

mosque A building in which Muslims worship.

nomad Someone who wanders from place to place, usually seasonally, to search for food and water or pasture for livestock.

oasis (plural: oases) Fertile ground in a desert where the level of underground water rises to or near ground level, and where plants grow and travelers can replenish water supplies.

peninsula A narrow piece of land that juts out from the mainland into an area of water.

people's republic A Socialist or Communist republic.

pilgrimage A religious journey to a holy place, undertaken for religious reasons.

poacher Someone who hunts or fishes illegally.

reform A change and improvement; the reorganization and improvement of something such as a political institution or system that is considered to be ineffective or unjust.

repression The process of suppressing a population, or the condition of having political, social, or cultural freedom controlled by force or military means.

republic A political system or form of government in which people elect representatives to exercise power for them.

steppe A vast, usually treeless plain, often dry and grass-covered.

subcontinent The area encompassing the countries of India, Pakistan, and Bangladesh, regarded as a distinct part of South Asia.

subsoil The soil beneath the topsoil.

Taliban Pashtun word meaning "religious student," the Taliban is an oppressive Islamist movement that ruled most of Afghanistan from 1996 to 2001, despite diplomatic recognition from only three countries, and that forged an alliance with Al Qaeda.

tsunami A large destructive ocean wave that is caused by an underwater earthquake or another movement of the Earth's surface.

woolly mammoth An extinct mammoth with a shaggy coat, small ears, and a thick layer of fat that lived during the Ice Age, native to cold regions of North America, Europe, and Asia.

yurt A collapsible circular tent made of felt and skins stretched over a pole frame in which Mongolian nomads live.

FOR MORE INFORMATION

Asian Art Museum
200 Larkin Street
San Francisco, CA 94102
(415) 581-3500
Web site: http://www.asianart.org
One of the largest museums in the Western world that is devoted to Asian art, this collection works toward leading a diverse global audience in discovering the achievements of Asian art and culture.

Asia Society
725 Park Avenue at Seventieth Street
New York, NY 10021
(212) 288-6400
Web site: http://www.asiasociety.org
This society is the leading organization working to strengthen relationships and encourage understanding among the people of Asia and the United States.

Association for Asian Studies
1021 East Huron Street
Ann Arbor, MI 48104
(734) 665-2490
Web site: http://www.aasianst.org
This organization has more than 7,000 members worldwide, and works to increase understanding of East, South, and Southeast Asia.

Freer Gallery of Art/Arthur M. Sackler Gallery
Smithsonian Institution
P.O. Box 37012, MRC 707
Washington , DC 20013-7012
(202) 633-1000

Web site: http://www.asia.si.edu
This gallery houses a collection of art from China, Japan, Korea, South and Southeast Asia, and the Near East.

National Geographic Society
P.O. Box 98199
Washington, DC 20090-8199
(800) 647-5463
Web site: http://www.nationalgeographic.com
This nonprofit scientific and educational institution encourages understanding of geography, archeology, natural science and environmental and historical conservation and the study of culture and history. The site offers information about Asia at http://travel.nationalgeographic.complaces/continents/continent_asia.html

WEB SITES

Due to the changing nature of Internet links, Rosen Publishing has developed an online list of Web sites related to the subject of this book. This site is updated regularly. Please use this link to access the list:

http://www.rosenlinks.com/atl/asia

FOR FURTHER READING

Aretha, David. *Discovering Asia's Land, People, and Wildlife* (Continents of the World). Berkeley Heights, NJ: Enslow Publishers, Inc., 2004.

Benhart, John E., and George M. Pomeroy. *South Asia* (Modern World Cultures). New York, NY: Chelsea House Publishers, 2005.

DiPiazza, Francesca. *Malaysia in Pictures* (Visual Geography Series). Minneapolis, MN: Twenty-First Century Books, 2006.

Fry, Gerald W. *The Association of Southeast Asian Nations* (Global Organizations). New York, NY: Chelsea House Publishers, 2008.

Goldstein, Margaret J. *Cambodia in Pictures* (Visual Geography Series). Minneapolis, MN: Twenty-First Century Books, 2004.

Kort, Michael. *The Handbook of East Asia* (The Handbook of…). Minneapolis, MN: Twenty-First Century Books, 2006.

Phillips, Douglas A. *East Asia* (Modern World Cultures). New York, NY: Chelsea House Publishers, 2005.

Phillips, Douglas A. *Southeast Asia* (Modern World Cultures). New York, NY: Chelsea House Publishers, 2005.

Sebag-Montefiore, Hugh. *China* (Eyewitness Books). New York, NY: Dorling Kindersley, 2007.

Stewart, Gail B. *Catastrophe in Southern Asia*: The Tsunami of 2004. Farmington Hills, MI: Lucent Books, 2005.

Streissguth, Tom. *Bangladesh in Pictures* (Visual Geography Series). Minneapolis, MN: Twenty-First Century Books, 2009.

Streissguth, Tom. *Myanmar in Pictures* (Visual Geography Series). Minneapolis, MN: Twenty-First Century Books, 2008.

Woods, Michael, and Mary B. Woods. *Seven Wonders of Ancient Asia* (Seven Wonders). Minneapolis, MN: Twenty-First Century Books, 2009.

INDEX

ABOUT THE AUTHORS

Rusty Campbell is a writer who lives in White Plains, New York.

Malcolm Porter is a leading cartographer for children's books. He has contributed to the *Times Atlas* and *Reader's Digest Atlas*, and has provided maps for leading educational and trade publishers. He drew the maps and designed the award-winning books *Atlas of the United States of America* and the *Collins Children's Atlas*.

Keith Lye is a best-selling author of geography titles for children of all ages. He is a distinguished contributor and consultant to major encyclopedias, including *Encyclopaedia Britannica* and *World Book*.

PICTURE CREDITS

Photographs: David Scott 26, 42
The Hutchison Library 8, 13, 15, 17, 21, 22, 23, 34, 35, 36